YHWH:

Order of the Divine NAME

James H. Kurt

© 2008, 2019 James H. Kurt
All Rights Reserved.

Children of Light Publications 11/30/2019
ISBN: 978-1-7332154-6-6

First published by AuthorHouse 2/14/2008
(ISBN: 978-1-4343-6865-2)

No part of this book may be reproduced, stored in a retrieval system, or transmitted by any means without the written permission of the author.

Nihil Obstat:
Rev. Donald Blumenfeld
Censor Librorum

Imprimatur:
+ Most Reverend John J. Myers, J.C.D., D.D.
Archbishop of Newark, New Jersey
December 5, 2007

The **Nihil Obstat** and **Imprimatur** are official declarations that a book or pamphlet is free of doctrinal error. No implication is contained therein that those who have granted the **Nihil Obstat** and **Imprimatur** agree with the contents, opinions, or statements expressed.

"I AM WHO I AM…
This is my NAME for ever."
Ex.3:14,15

"…and after the fire
a still small voice..."
1Kgs.19:12

"Be still,
and know that I am God."
Ps.46:10

"Open your mouth wide,
and I will fill it."
Ps.81:11

Author's Preface

When Moses asks the Lord His Name (upon being called by Him to lead the Israelites out of slavery in Egypt – see Exodus 3), the Lord gives His chosen one three answers:

1) "YHWH" – His silent, awe-inspiring NAME
(not even recorded in many Bibles);

2) "I AM" / "I AM WHO (I) AM" –
interpretation/explanation of His NAME that we might understand it;

3) "the God of Abraham, the God of Isaac, and the God of Jacob" –
who He is in relation to man.

Here are three levels: the first is the most profound and necessary; the other two, though useful to discover the first, fall short of expressing God's being.

The third is how the Israelites came primarily to understand Him – as the Father of Abraham, whose favored flesh and blood descendents they were. But as the Baptist has said: "God is able from these stones to raise up children to Abraham" (Mt.3:9), so relating to God on this level is not sufficient for knowing and becoming one with Him.

The second indeed serves as explanation, as interpretation… as words to help comprehend the Word Himself. This is all well and good. But one can have all kinds of words about God and yet not know God at all, as is the case with many scholars, as was the case with the Pharisees. For Jesus told the Pharisees: "You search the scriptures, because you think that in them you have eternal life; and it is they that bear witness to me; yet you refuse to come to me that you may have life" (Jn.5:39-40).

The first, to which all must come to know the Lord truly and have life, is His NAME itself, YHWH (not Yahweh or Jehovah or any other variation): His silent NAME… a Name, a Word, which silences all words, all tongues, and in which all things, all attachments to this world, pass away. His NAME is means He gives to coming into His presence, which is always with us and to which He always calls us. It is this Word which became flesh in Jesus the Christ, who fully reveals God's presence to us. (One might say God revealed His "back" (see Ex.33:23) in His NAME given to Moses, whereas Jesus reveals the very face of God.)

This book on the Divine NAME and an order of life founded upon it is a prayer for all to be released from slavery to words, to things of the world, to blindness and sin… and come into the Lord's presence as His children. Essentially, it asks whether it is sufficient to confine ourselves to saying of the Father's Divine NAME that it is too sacred to be pronounced, whether this may not constitute a kind of avoidance of realization of a great gift He has provided to man – and in the end whether such "ignorance" of the Father does not keep us from fully knowing the Son, and the gift of God's presence He is to us (the face He came to reveal).

Should we not speak the Father's NAME in the holy of holies with us now in every Catholic Church, that is, before the Blessed Sacrament? Should we not come into the Lord's presence wherever we are?

God love you and be with you.

Introduction

I believe there is a certain significance to this work, to the understanding of the NAME it seeks to convey, and the graces that are wrought in its speaking. The great mystics speak often of the wordless wonder of being in God's presence, of His peace which passes understanding and the great blessing of unity with Him… but none I've read has connected coming into His awe-inspiring Presence with the speaking of His NAME. (Few have even noted the great gift the Blessed Sacrament is to mystical awareness of the Lord.)

Some have spoken of the NAME as the giving of a name and yet a refusal of a name. Pope Benedict XVI in his book *Jesus of Nazareth* calls the NAME "enigmatic" and the statement "I AM WHO I AM" "equally enigmatic" (p. 347). Yet though he clarifies well the significance of "I AM" ("He just *is*, without any qualification" (ibid)), the Holy Father does not seek to address the significance of the NAME itself, of these four letters (though one must say he touches upon it elsewhere when he defines prayer as "being in silent inward communion with God" (p. 130).)

I do not really know what I do here. Can it be that what God gave to Moses as an everlasting remembrance has been so seriously forgotten? It does not seem possible that such a perfectly simple thing, a childlike comprehension, could be unknown for so many centuries, if not millennia. Do I here rediscover the significance – the pronunciation – of God's NAME? Is it already well understood? Or do I err somehow in my interpretation?

I can but offer these writings for the edification of the Lord's children.

Table of Contents

I. YHWH: The Divine NAME 1

   1. YHWH: "I AM WHO I AM"
      (a short poem) 3

   2. YHWH: On the NAME of God
      (a long poem) 7

   3. YHWH (an essay) 34

   4. YHWH: "Remember My NAME"
      (a longer essay) 41

   5. On Speaking the NAME: A Caveat 52

II. Toward an Order 53

   1. *I Am...* 57

   2. Hermit in the City 85

   3. "You Are My Tabernacle" 107

   4. Order of the Divine NAME
      (with Horarium) 123

III. Into Practice 135

   1. Sylvia 139

   2. A Third Pilgrimage 173

   3. A Married Hermit 183

IV. On Finding a House of Prayer 189

   1. Four Hours 193

   2. Striving 207

This work is ostensibly a compilation of writings composed over the course of about twenty years. They are grouped into four chronological sections. The first is a series – two poems and two essays – on the NAME itself. The second contains writings on the development of a spiritual life based on the Divine NAME. The third presents compositions about putting the life into loving practice; and, finally, there are notes reflecting a striving to find a House of Prayer in the Church.

> **"Silence is so powerful a language
> that it reaches the throne of the living God.
> Silence is His language."**
>
> St. Faustina
> (*Diary*, Notebook II, #888)

I

YHWH:
The Divine NAME

1. **YHWH: "I AM WHO I AM"**
   (a short poem)
2. **YHWH: On the NAME of God**
   (a long poem)
3. **YHWH** (an essay)
4. **YHWH: "Remember My NAME"**
   (a longer essay)
5. **On Speaking the NAME: A Caveat**

An Introduction to the NAME

Though conscious consideration of the Divine NAME began in 1986 upon reading of discovery of an ancient Israelite priest's vestment, which had the NAME on the front and the Aaronic blessing on the back, I had written a song two years before that intuitively reflected the understanding later gained. I had been walking through the park one evening, seeking the Lord and to speak with Him, to find His presence, by naming the things around me one by one, ending with the words "God" and "Father"… when I found myself in absolute silence, lips pursed but with no word to express His wonder upon me. Here are the lyrics of the song (taken from *Breath, The Apple Rises*, fifth album of *Songs for Children of Light*):

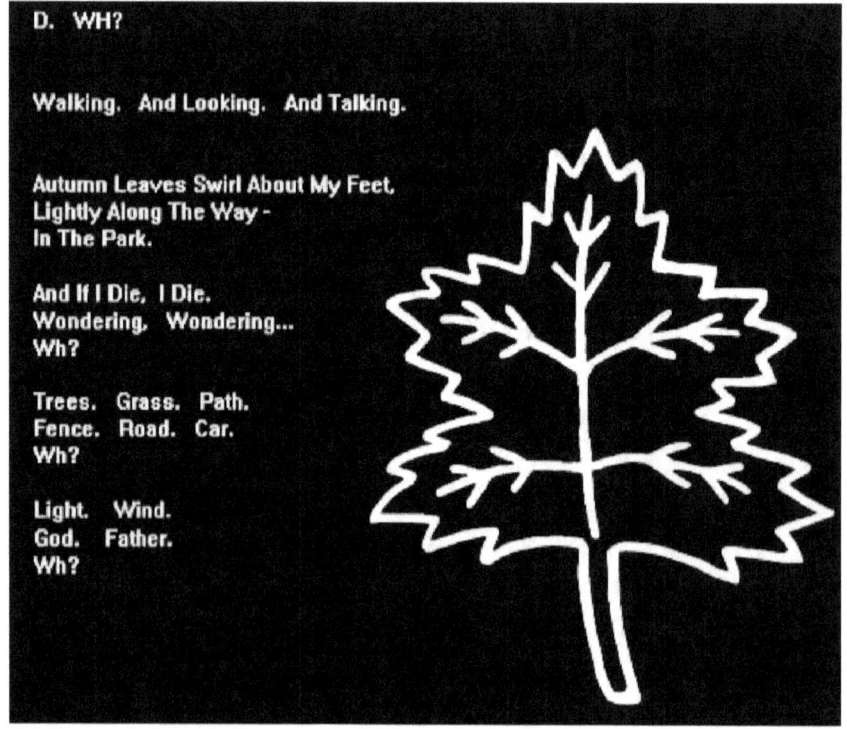

D. WH?

Walking. And Looking. And Talking.

Autumn Leaves Swirl About My Feet,
Lightly Along The Way -
In The Park.

And If I Die, I Die.
Wondering. Wondering…
Wh?

Trees. Grass. Path.
Fence. Road. Car.
Wh?

Light. Wind.
God. Father.
Wh?

I thus happened upon the speaking of the NAME quite ingenuously.

1.

YHWH:

"I AM WHO I AM"

(a short poem)

© 1992 James H. Kurt

(excerpted from *The Four Corners of the Universe*)

I. YHWH: The Divine NAME

And of the holy NAME of God,
the Word that was
in the beginning,
the Word that became Man
in Jesus Christ...

Of what significance is this
four-letter NAME – YHWH?

It is the silent Word,
the Word of words,
the Tongue of tongues –
the Word which allows
the passage of air
through the human being,
undefiled by his humanness...

The Word of pure Spirit,
the NAME of God,
which cannot be subject
to any human tongue.

1. YHWH: "I AM WHO AM"

And yet it is a word,
with four letters
so arranged
as to defy pronunciation
and yet allow air
to pass through us.

Physically, the "Y"
poises the mouth for speech –
but the "H" immediately
opens the throat,
preventing enunciation.
Then, as the lips approach
one another ("W"),
perhaps to ask a question...
they are left open
by the final "H".

I. YHWH: The Divine NAME

And one is left
in a state of pure wonder,
sensing the presence of God
within oneself,
and all around oneself.

One is filled with the innocence
and purity
of God's beauty.

Thus one may come
to know God
by simply speaking
His silent NAME.

(Be as a child
before his Father.)

2.

Y H W H

On the NAME of God

(a long poem)

© 1995

James H. Kurt

I. YHWH: The Divine NAME

    Breathe in and breathe out,
        and you shall be speaking
            the NAME of God.

    With mouth agape
        and no words other
    than this pure breath,

        you shall know
        His presence.

    The life of the Spirit taken in,
        the offering of your life given out –
    you shall be as one with Him.

    And this Word is the source of all life;
        in this Word is the kingdom of heaven...

    And so a NAME is given to that
        which is only spiritual,
      a Word is provided for us to speak –

    that we might come into His presence,
        that we might know the life of God.

2. YHWH: On the NAME of God

I

With mouth agape,
    we worship the one and only God –
    we speak His holy NAME.

In this pure breathing,
    in this complete breath...
    is found the truth of life –
    is found life itself.

And the great I AM is present to us
    in this breathing,
    in this truth.
  The holy Lord approaches us
    as we speak His NAME.

Yes, this pure breathing,
    which fills us to our fingertips
        and toes,
    is a language all its own...
It is the invincible power of God made known.

And as we sit still and worship Him,
    as He breathes His Spirit into our skin –
    so we are made one with Him.

I. YHWH: The Divine NAME

One with Him we are made aware
of the life which surrounds us.
Breathing as one with the Spirit of God,
the life it is within us.

Into our nostrils He breathes the breath of life,
our hearts He sets on fire
with His holy love.
And even as we breathe,
clearly as we speak,
the closer to the truth we come –
the more we are made as His Son.

For the more we come to know His NAME,
founded in this breath,
the more we shall come to know Him.
And coming to know Him,
we will be like Him...
even as His Son.

So breathe in, and breathe out –
even as God intended.
Live according to His Spirit of life,
and so your soul you shall find.

2. YHWH: On the NAME of God

Penetrate deep within us, O Lord.
  Your NAME separates
    even soul and spirit;
   it cuts to the marrow of our bone.
The NAME of God spoken within us
    searches our thoughts
    and our intentions.
  With its sacred fire it purges
    the dark spots
    of our immortal souls:
   it renews us and makes us whole.

The Word of God will convict you,
   it will go deep within you –
 O Lord, let that Word indeed restore our souls.

Breathing in and breathing out
  in the light of Christ,
  yielding to the sacred Spirit
   all our unholy lives...
calling on the NAME of God
  to take all words uttered by our tongue,
 we shall indeed be redeemed once more –
  the truth shall make us whole.

I. YHWH: The Divine NAME

> Truth is what lives in Him,
>> it is all that is spoken
>>> in His NAME.
> The Word is filled, it billows forth,
>> only with the light of truth,
>> only with the Holy Spirit.

> God, Father,
>> may your NAME be hallowed
>> by the souls of all;
> may your Word be upon the tongue
>> of all your chosen sons.
> Write your Law upon our hearts;
>> let us breathe only in your light.
>>> Let every word we speak be true:
>>> let all our thoughts be right.

> In reverence and truth
>> we sit silently before our God,
>> and speak His NAME with silent tongues –
>>> in silence He touches our hearts.

> The Word of God it makes no sound;
>> for His NAME our lips they do but part.

2. YHWH: On the NAME of God

Wonder, pure wonder,
    and nothing more,
      comes upon us
        when we speak
          the NAME of God.
When we breathe with His pure breath,
    a breath unadulterated by words,
      unhindered by our humanness,
        unlimited by our tongues –
then the flame of His pure light
    pierces our minds,
    and purges all our thoughts.

With no trace of corruption remaining
    to constrain our souls,
all we know is He Who Is –
    what is and will ever be.

And from this state we speak in tongues,
    for tongues of the Spirit are all that is useful
      when our own language
        becomes so pale –
tongues of wonder are all that can say
    what cannot be said by man.

I. YHWH: The Divine NAME

11

Yes, He is present
    as we speak His holy NAME;
  in the silence He speaks to us
      and reveals to us His Person.

Christ who lives in all that is
    is made apparent to our eyes
  as we open our hearts
    to His Spirit.

The Word of the Father entering our being
    and finding our soul's surrender,
  we are thus filled with His Holy Spirit
    and living life with Jesus.

Open your mouth in awe to Him;
    open the eyes of your mind as a child.
  An open heart will sense His touch,
      so your soul will be blessed by His Spirit.

Our jaws drop as He comes to us;
    tears begin to fill our eyes...
  and so we are purged in His light.

2. YHWH: On the NAME of God

The Spirit of Christ is present in all things.
    The Word of the Father passes through
        all the universe.
    The love of God it is that lives
        and sustains all life.

This we come to know by dwelling in His presence.
    This we come to know breathing His holy NAME.
        Our Father, who is in heaven,
        comes to us in our silent prayer.

He fills us. He draws us forth.
    He blesses us with light.
    And so we become His children,
        His children of light.

For the more we sit at His holy feet,
    the more we draw water from His well...
    the more we will come to know the Father –
        the more we will live His Gospel.

Know the presence of God within yourself;
    live in its light here on earth.

I. YHWH: The Divine NAME

    As awesome wonder fills our souls,
        we are lifted up to the Lord;
    our eyes shine with His light
        as we offer our lives to Him.

Becoming one with our God,
    all else falls away.
For this is all we need,
    to be in His holy presence;
this is all that matters now –
    to be washed in His light.

Transcendence of this world comes
    as we enter in to Him;
we are lifted to His throne
    as we cast aside our sin.

Reunion with the Father of all,
    the Father who is love,
    is made apparent and complete
        through belief in His only Son.

And this wonder is all we need
    to unite with the heart of love.

2. YHWH: On the NAME of God

Praise God and live your life –
   breathe in His pure light...
  Alleluia, we sing to Jesus,
     as in the Lord's Word we dwell.

The Word made flesh, our very brother –
   Jesus is the Image of God.
  In His light we live on this earth,
     and again in the life to come.

O God, our Father,
   thank you for the gift of your Son.
O God, our Father,
   that He has made your Word known.

Our God and Father gave to Moses His NAME;
   the Lord spoke to His servant so humble.
And so entrusted to us was this bond with God,
   for by His NAME we came to know Him.

And now that knowledge has been fulfilled,
   in the coming of His Son –
now that breath is made complete,
   and victory over this world is won.

I. YHWH: The Divine NAME

    The presence of the Lord
        is made known in His Word.
    The Word is spoken in the Son.

    Speak to us in silence, O Lord of all;
        let your Word become our very
            flesh and blood.
    Speaking to you, we are set free –
        let us speak to you with all our lives.

    The Lord will write His NAME upon your hearts.
        He will come to you and make you
            His sons.
    There will be no need to fear;
        no confusion shall touch your minds.

    Minds of light, we are clear as glass,
        seeing into His holy sphere.
    No words other than His pure breath,
        there now are no questions asked.

    And so we hope to live forever,
        as children of His light.

2. YHWH: On the NAME of God

III

In the beginning,
the Father breathed upon man –
    and so he became a living soul.
After His resurrection,
Jesus breathed upon the disciples –
    and so they were born again.

The Spirit of life has returned to us
    who would receive His holy call.
  The joy of new life
      and the glory of God
        are granted
to those who would listen to the Lord.

And as we respond to His voice,
    as we answer this call of the Lord...
as we offer in return our lives –
    with the Father we are made one
      once more.

The disciples were quick to speak
  in the NAME of the Lord.
    Breathing in the Holy Spirit,
      they could but give their lives for all.

I. YHWH: The Divine NAME

And the breath of the Spirit is beyond words.
The breath of the Spirit is a language
all its own.
The breath of the Spirit leaves our mouths
hanging open –
it leaves our lips ever pursed.

For the breath of the Spirit cannot be constrained
by any human tongue.
The breath of the Spirit is far above
our human thinking,
our human speaking...
it is not within the limits of our mind.

The breath of the Spirit is pure.
The breath of the Spirit is the source
of life.
The Word of God is spoken with
the breath of the Spirit.

And no human words have any life
without the Word of God.
Nothing has meaning without
the breath of the Spirit.
The Spirit is in all that is alive.

2. YHWH: On the NAME of God

That is all there is,
   this breathing in and breathing out
   in the life of the Spirit.

That is all there is;
   it is all that matters now.
All power and glory come
     from the breath of God.

The I AM, the God and Father
     of all,
   is known to us
in the power of His Word.

And He is what He will be,
   He is all that is –
We cannot place our finger
   upon the pulse of God;
we can but live with Him.

So, let us breathe in the acceptance
     of His Spirit,
   the illumination of our minds –
and breathe out the offering of our lives.

I. YHWH: The Divine NAME

> No other God is there but Him,
>> and so, no other place should we go.
>> And so, never should we hesitate
>>> to trust in His holy light.

> I love you, Lord;
>> come in and dwell with me.
> Breathe your Spirit down upon me,
>> that I might truly be free.

> Fill me with thy Holy Spirit,
>> let His tongue of fire
>> alight upon my mind.
> Let the flame of wisdom
>> open my eyes –
>> take my unholy life.

> I offer you my heart and soul now.
>> I lift my hands up to your NAME.
> You lift my head to look upon you;
>> you shine upon me the light of your face.

> Hayah... Hayah... Hayah...
> O Lord, let me be in your presence!

2. YHWH: On the NAME of God

Holy, Holy, Holy
   is the Lord Jesus!
  The glory of the Lord
    shines all about us.

Alleluia! Alleluia! Alleluia!
   We shall live in the Word of God.
  Praise be to our Lord and Savior;
    praise be the light of God!

He gives us life.
He breathes upon us.
  In His Word we live
    and are free.
His Spirit which does fall upon us
   enlightens us in the knowledge
    of God.

Yes, the Lord grants us
   His holy inspiration,
  and we offer our hearts
    on the altar of God.

And so we become one in the glory of light.

IV

    Life is breathed forth by the Word
        of God.
    God speaks, and things come to be.

    The source of all Creation is found
        in the Word of God.

    This is God.
    God is life.
    This is what God is.

    There is no death in God.
    There is no darkness in God –
        in God there is no sin.

    And this is what the Son of Man
        has shown us.
    This is what the Son of Man
        has brought to earth.

    The Word of God has dwelt among us.
        He has shown us the life that is.
        He has brought the kingdom of God
            into our midst.

2. YHWH: On the NAME of God

God is.
Simply this and nothing more –
    God is.

God.   YHWH.   The WORD.
    I AM.
  God is. The Father breathes.
    Life comes to be.

And the source of all goodness
    and healing
      is His Son,
        the Lord Jesus Christ,
who by His sinless sacrifice
has shown us the way
    to the Father.

The way to life is by Jesus Christ.
    The kingdom of God resides
      in His flesh and bone.
  And as we eat His body,
    as we drink His blood...
  as we become one with Him,
    so to us the kingdom becomes known.

I. YHWH: The Divine NAME

    The kingdom of God is in our midst.
      It dwells here now with us.
    In the power of the Spirit
        Christ has left
      the means to discover His life.

Look around yourself.
Open up your eyes.
See with eyes made new by His blood.
Breathe with the Spirit of Christ.

The Spirit of Wisdom shall come upon you.
The light of the Lord shall come
      to your heart.
You shall be made new from head to toe.
    You shall be alive once more.

There is no mystery to the presence
      of Christ.
  It is plain as day.
The Spirit of the Lord breathes life into all things;
    His glory is existent throughout
      this land.

2. YHWH: On the NAME of God

Come to us, Lord Jesus,
>   living Word of God.
> Reveal to us your presence;
>   let us know that you are God.

The Father dwells with the Son;
>   He and the Father are one.
> And through them the Holy Spirit goes forth
>   and fills the heart of all.

And the life of God comes to earth,
>   where it has ever been.
> And so renewal is offered to us,
>   to save us from our sin.

Jesus saves.
God lives and Jesus saves.
The Father breathes,
>   the Spirit gives life –
>   and Jesus is that life.

Know you are a brother to Jesus –
>   understand you are the Father's son.

I. YHWH: The Divine NAME

No further need have we
    than to call upon the NAME
        of the Lord.
All we require will be given us
    in the Word of God.

It is the Father's good pleasure
    to give to us.
He wishes all the glory of His kingdom
    to be with us even now.

And so we need only believe
    and ask of Him
and all will be revealed to us.

This is the gift Jesus has given us,
    to have means to address the Father.
He has come to tell of the Father's love
    and the life that awaits us in Him.

The Lord has come to remind us
    of what we have forgot –
that life is in God and we are called
    to be His sons.

V

Communication occurs only in the Spirit.
And communication with God is
    purely spiritual.
Communication occurs only in silence,
and in silence is spoken the Word of God.

Beyond any human tongue God speaks,
    and only in its stillness
        do we begin to perceive
           who God is.

And God leads us to this stillness
    by His blessed NAME.
The Lord gives us letters to follow
    to find the source of all letters,
        to find the Spirit of all words.

He allows us to enter into His presence
    and become one with His Spirit
        by the gift of this Word:

YHWH.
This is the Word that shall silence your tongue;
this is the NAME of the Holy One.

I. YHWH: The Divine NAME

    YHWH.
    It cannot be pronounced, some say...
        and this is so.
    (And if it cannot be pronounced there is no question
        about whether or not it should.)
    For it is silent.

    And yet the silence it brings is so palpable
        as to possess all words
            of every language –
    it is the source of the Spirit tongue.

    And speaking in this tongue
        all is understood.
    For all is infused with the light of wisdom;
        all possesses the power of God
            when His silent NAME
                is upon our tongues.

    Leading us away from all words,
        it leads us to the Word,
        and all the meaning contained therein.
    Bathing us in silence, it opens our ears
        to the Spirit of all communication.

2. YHWH: On the NAME of God

A paradox is this NAME of God,
    this Word from which all comes.
   For though beyond all tongues
      and finding life only in the Spirit –
yet it is writ in letters our tongues may know.

And so by human means we may come
    to that which is purely spiritual.

This is a great gift from God.
This shows His power,
    and also His mercy:
   though it be far beyond our understanding,
    He teaches us of His great glory
      in a way He knows
      we may understand.

This gift is fulfilled in the coming of Christ;
    in the presence of Jesus
      we find this Word made flesh –
   we find ourselves fully refreshed
     in His blood.
And the gift to Moses foreshadows this;
    it indicates the presence of our God.

I. YHWH: The Divine NAME

Speak the NAME of God.
Form the letters as they are written,
   and your mind shall be opened
      to His presence.

"YHWH".
Open your throat with the "Y",
   and leave it so with the "H".
(Thus the Spirit may enter you.)

Your mouth hanging open,
   you may move your lips toward a question ("W"),
      but never let them touch ("H").
(And so you offer your life.)

Yes, let the wind of the Spirit
   breathe into you...
    breathe out with the Spirit of God.
Let the pure breath of the Spirit
   fan the lamp of your mind.

And so you shall become a child of light;
   so you shall come to know God.

2. YHWH: On the NAME of God

I cannot say what insight
    this realization has given me.
Though I remain sinful,
    yet the Lord blesses me.
He remains with me through all trial.

I encourage all His children
    to keep holy the NAME of God,
    to watch their tongues and all they speak –
and subjugate themselves to the silence of the Lord.

The Father has given you His holy NAME;
    He has told you who He Is.
And He has shown this in totality
    in the flesh and blood of Jesus.

Turn you not from His light.
Forsake not His holy words.

Come into His presence and glorify Him;
    sit in awe in His holy NAME.

© 1996 James H. Kurt

3.

YHWH

(an essay)

In this essay we will seek to discover the very essence of the Bible – whose very name means the Book – and so the significance of God's NAME: YHWH. For what is a book but words? And what are words but spirit? And this Word (YHWH) is the pure expression of the Spirit, of God – it is the NAME of God, the Word itself.

Let me begin by saying that all is by words, and all comes from God. God is the origin; God is the source of all.

The Bible tells us that in the beginning God breathed the breath of life into the nostrils of man, and so he became "a living soul" (Gn.2:7). The breath is the life of the soul, and our words are its expression; breathing in and breathing out, we find the source of the words we speak. And the words I speak of are not only the audible words we use when conversing with one another, but, more importantly, the words we speak inside… for these, our thoughts, come from deeper in our souls.

You have no doubt heard the expression, "You are what you eat." This is certainly true of the body: the food we eat becomes our flesh. (And so should we not eat the flesh of Christ?) But as for the soul, it is equally true that *you are what you speak*, for a man is judged by his words.

Yes, all is by words, all occurs as a result of the words we speak. Even the most astounding action performed by man has its source in words, for actions spring from words – we act according to our thoughts.

And this is why there is no greater power than the power of prayer – sincere, true words, spoken in the Spirit of God may indeed move mountains. This is why Jesus says, "If you have faith the size of a mustard seed, you would say to this mulberry tree, 'Be uprooted and planted in the sea,' and it would obey you" (Lk.17:6). Speak in truth and it shall be done.

3. YHWH (an essay)

Let us now speak of the Spirit. The Word. God. The source of all life... And of His NAME: YHWH.

Jesus tells us that God is Spirit, and the Spirit is like the wind. He says that the words He speaks are Spirit and life – but what does He mean? (See Jn.3:8, 4:24, & 6:63.)

Some may recognize this Word – YHWH – as being similar to the Name 'Yahweh', one name for God. But Yahweh is a much later version of the NAME, with vowels arbitrarily added in. The original form of the NAME is this Word, YHWH. It is called the tetragrammaton. There are other derivations and names for God – like Jehovah and Adonai, or Lord – but this is the original NAME.

This NAME was revealed to Moses at the burning bush when God called him to lead the Israelites out of Egyptian slavery. God gave the NAME to Moses that he might know God and be confident in speaking to the Israelites, and that they might know who sent him. This NAME is a lasting gift for all generations (surpassed only by the coming of Christ – the Word become flesh).

This NAME is translated in the Bible as "I AM WHO (I) AM," simply as "I AM," or as "I WILL BE WHAT I WILL BE," and it is said to be related to the Hebrew verb "hayah," which means "to be". These interpretations are very enlightening about the nature of God. They tell us, simply, that God Is, God exists; He is life and the Creator and Master of life – able to do and be what He will.

These definitions lead us to an understanding of the nature of God as Life itself: but still, I wonder when I look at this NAME – what is its significance? I asked this question of the Spirit in 1986 after reading that archeologists had unearthed a priest's vestment (circa 500 B.C.) with these four letters on the front and the Aaronic blessing on the back.

I had read that no one was certain of the significance of this Word. All scholars could say was that either it could not be pronounced or should not be pronounced... but they were not sure. Going on this alone, and with the simplicity of a child, I thought, in the Spirit, to pronounce it – as it is, without the added vowels.

I. YHWH: The Divine NAME

What I found, miraculously, was a word whose pronunciation is silence itself. A word that leads to no words. It defies pronunciation, and yet has a pronunciation – its pronunciation is silence... living, breathing silence!

It is a word of pure breath, for it allows air – air that is of the wind, that is of the spirit – to pass through us without any human interference, without any movement of tongue or lips or vocal cords... And so I found that it is the Word of words, the Tongue of tongues, the Spirit, the Breath that is in all words, in all languages – it is the silence from which all words come.

And I thought of that ancient priest standing in a field, looking at the dome of clouds overhead, listening to the wind in the trees – and just breathing, just being – one with nature and with God, no words or thoughts to trouble him... the purity of the Spirit filling him.

In speaking the NAME, you will find that the "Y" opens the throat and poises the mouth for speech, but the "H" immediately leaves it open – allowing the spirit, the breath, to enter in purely and fill the mind with light. (This is breathing in the pure Spirit of God.)

Then, with the "W" the lips move toward one another, as if to ask a question – but are left open by the final "H". (And so we breathe out and offer our lives to God, released from all question, doubt, and fear.)

And we are left in utter awe and wonder – with mouth agape and tongue quite still – as a smiling child before the Father and His inexpressible beauty, majesty, and love.

(It is important to note that at the same time God gives us His NAME, He lets us know that we cannot put our finger on Him; we, as His creation, as His clay pots, cannot in human ways, with a human tongue, name God – for God is beyond our words: God simply Is.)

3. YHWH (an essay)

Now, let us found this understanding in the Word of God.

First, let us look at 1Kings 19:9-18. In this passage, Elijah listens for the Lord on Mount Horeb and finds Him not in the strong wind that rends the mountain in two, nor in the earthquake, nor in the fire – but in a "still small voice." (And after hearing this voice, Elijah rises, and God commissions him to anoint two kings and a prophet.)

Next, let us discuss two pairs of related readings, taken from the Old and New Testaments:

First, in Genesis (1:1,2) we read, "In the beginning God created the heavens and the earth. The earth was without form and void, and darkness was upon the face of the deep." Nothing had taken shape yet, but the Bible tells us that "the Spirit [or wind] of God was moving over the face of the waters." So, all that was in the beginning was this Spirit, this wind, this breath of God.

And then, what happens? – God speaks. "God said, 'Let there be light'; and there was light" (1:3). And so all things come into being by the Word of God. So nothing becomes something by the Word of God, the origin of life.

Related to this passage is the beginning of the Gospel of John, which reads, "In the beginning was the Word, and the Word was with God, and the Word was God." Again, the Word is the origin. The Spirit gives life. God is the Spirit, the Word.

John goes on to tell us that Jesus is the Word, is God, made flesh. He is the Word become Man; He is the Son of God the Father – the light of the world. And so the revelation given Moses is fulfilled in Jesus, as Spirit becomes flesh.

As for the other pair of relevant readings: to emphasize again the importance of breath and its relation to God, I remind you that Genesis tells us that God breathed the breath of life into man's nostrils, and so he became a living being. This is the first birth.

Then I draw your attention to a passage directly related to this one – that which speaks of the second birth. And what is it to be born again, to be born from above, to be, as Jesus told Nicodemus, like the wind of which no one knows "whence it comes or whither it goes" (Jn.3:8)? We see a clear parallel to the first birth in John 20, when the risen Christ commissions the apostles: He breathes on them, first saying, "Peace be with you," then, "Receive the Holy Spirit" (19, 22). And so the Church is born of the Spirit (even as it is in its fullness at Pentecost, when the wind of the Spirit shakes the house in which the apostles pray, and comes upon them in tongues of living flame).

In closing, I would like to say that I believe the understanding of the NAME of God as the silent Word may have been lost due to the impatience and weariness of the people. I believe that the NAME warranted a silent pause whenever it appeared in the Scriptures being read aloud in the assembly and that people's ears and hearts grew dull to this pure silence, and so words more understandable and pronounceable – more human – were added in its place.

I pray we are not the same as they. I pray that we will find the great life in the silence of God, in His holy NAME – not tediousness or emptiness. And so I greatly encourage you to pray to God to find the still point of the turning world, to find His silence, His silent Word from which all comes and which holds all life. Give yourselves over to His wonder and awe. Be still and listen for His voice, which speaks in all words and is at the heart of all sound. Speak His NAME.

Peace be with you.

3. YHWH (an essay)

an epilogue

I have learned recently that the NAME came to be pronounced only by the high priest in the holy of holies, where the Ark of the Covenant was kept and which only he was allowed to enter, and only once a year. Perhaps, then, the NAME fell into disuse after the Ark was lost at the time of the Babylonian exile.

Also, two substantial notes regarding this practice and any proscriptions against speaking the NAME. First, it was part of the command given to Moses when the NAME was revealed to him, "This is my NAME for ever, and thus I am to be remembered throughout all generations" (Ex.3:15). How could we then forget it so? Second, the tabernacle housing the Blessed Sacrament, the fulfillment of the Ark of the Covenant, has indeed taken the place of the holy of holies; it is the place where God is now present to us – and it is now present in every Catholic Church throughout the world. And not only may anyone enter into that presence at any time, but any Catholic in a state of grace may receive that presence of God into his own body by reception of Holy Communion, even every day. How much more should His NAME be remembered now that the Word has become flesh and dwells among us? Let us remember His NAME.

I. YHWH: The Divine NAME

**"Let us listen to the voice of God;
let us enter into His rest."**

(Ordinary Invitatory Antiphon for Saturday of Week IV,
Office of Readings)

4.

YHWH:
"Remember My NAME"

"I AM WHO I AM…
this is my NAME forever,
and thus I am to be remembered
throughout all generations."

Ex.3:14,15

© 2001 James H. Kurt
(previously published in *Turn of the Jubilee Year*, 2004)

I. YHWH: The Divine NAME

Introductory Note

The title of this writing reflects a word given me by the Lord during a private Holy Hour in the chapel at Bethlehem Hermitage in Chester, New Jersey, in 2001. I had been seeking vocation direction from the Lord. The word came after His calling me to teach through writing. Here is an account of the experience from Five Days in the Desert (from *Turn of the Jubilee Year*, p. 144):

> The Lord then gave me a blessed command. First I heard it as "Remember my Word," but later He clarified it as "Remember my Name." And these words rang with holy, loving truth – and I could see His blessed lips forming them… His Word. His NAME. YHWH. His silence. His Presence. The revelation at the heart of my writing, and of my faith… And now in these days He lets me know that I am called to remember His NAME not only at certain times (or worse yet, in some merely intellectual way), but to speak this NAME – this NAME which is of life and love, a love embodied on the Cross – constantly. And I have but to open my mouth to do so.

This work is the last extended effort I made to explicate God's holy NAME, and may perhaps be the fullest.

4. YHWH: "Remember My NAME"

- I -

How does one explicate silence?
How does one tell of the NAME of God?

Let us begin by saying what it is not.

I. YHWH: The Divine NAME

1.

It is not darkness; it is not *death*.

> "It is not the nether world that gives you thanks,
> nor death that praises you."
> Is.38:18

It is appropriate that I begin this writing, and particularly this theme, on Holy Saturday (from whose Morning Prayer the above quote is taken), for on this day we know death most deeply; for on this day the Word is silenced. And this silence is not that of which I speak.

The silence we experience this day is the absence of the voice of God in the absence of the Son by whom we know the Word of the Father. It is the absence of life itself. This silence is death; but God is life. Such emptiness does not denote Him, but is indeed the inverse of what He is.

In speaking to the Sadducees, those who disbelieved the resurrection of the dead, Jesus tells us that God is not "God of the dead, but of the living" (Mt.22:32) – God has no store in death; it is the living who give Him thanks (see Is.38:19). This is a most important point as we start out on our treatise, for many there are who erroneously think death is a solution to the problems, the suffering of life: the solution is to speak, to pray, to call upon God's NAME and enter into His presence. Death can but intensify the state one is in; only in life release is found.

If I may be permitted a reference to a work of literature (not that Scripture is lacking illustrations of those who would call the rocks to fall upon themselves to end their suffering – see Rv.6:15-17, for example), in perhaps the most famous speech of Shakespeare's *Hamlet, Prince of Denmark*, the prince contemplates suicide to end his woes – "To be or not to be…" (3.1.56) – but realizes he cannot his own "quietus make" (75), that death will not guarantee his peace: "For in that sleep of death what dreams may come, when we have shuffled off this mortal coil" (66-67). Indeed, life, that which is in God's hands, is not so easily dispensed with, and the presumption of taking it in our own hands may bring us but an eternal death, an eternal suffering, wherein is no rest. We do not silence the voice of life by turning in vain to death, but we might by our own device make that voice estranged. (Indeed, as I have written elsewhere, the silence that is God's NAME is not like the laughter of aborted babies missing from our streets.)

2.

It is not mute; it is not the absence of sound.

In the same vein, this silence of which we speak is not without voice; it is far from the mere lack of sound, which would, in fact, be its denial. Though still, it moves – it moves all and is the source of all true sound, of all true words, and is known in and through them. Jesus came to us speaking; He came to us teaching… He came to us accomplishing the deeds of the Father, and it is the fruit of this tree we eat:

> "For thus says the Lord,
> the creator of the heavens,
> who is God,
> the designer and maker of the earth
> who established it,
> not creating it to be a waste,
> but designing it to be lived in:
> I am the Lord, and there is no other.
> I have not spoken from hiding
> nor from some dark place of the earth.
> And I have not said to the descendants of Jacob,
> 'Look for me in an empty waste.'"
> Is.45:18-19

He lives in light and in life, and His Word brings life. (Enter into that Word.)

This is significant because there are those, and in abundance, who think it best simply to keep their mouths closed, to turn a blind eye, to say nothing in the face of the evil and sin of this world – they think that such silence is of God. It is not. We are not born and given the gift of the tongue and the Word stirring in our hearts to be speechless, to be dumb. We are of the tree that is Jesus and must bear fruit accordingly. The Word of God is not of ignorance. This is not whence its silence comes. Indeed, it must be spoken.

Does Jonah do well to turn his face from Ninevah? Is it not for this he finds himself in the belly of the whale? Is it in that dark silence the Lord speaks? No, the light of God does not radiate in the whale's belly, as it does not radiate in the tomb – we cannot shut our mouths or turn away when the Lord calls us; we must ever speak in His Name. As He tells Ezekiel (see 33:7-9), in this will be our salvation, whether our audience listen or not. Yes, we must open our mouths and speak in His Name.

These two points are important in order to avoid the laziness which, along with pride, is the bane of the religious: instead of resting with the Lord, he might tend to fall asleep, thus failing to remain "awake" for the hour the Lord requests.

There is, however, a third point:

3.

It knows nothing of noise.

Silence. How can silence be of noise? Though the silent Word of God, His NAME, is spoken out for all to hear, though from it all true sound emanates, none of that sound is of noise – none of it is wasted expression.

The voice of God is as music, harmonious and whole, balanced and radiant. The voice of God sings in all sound and can only be heard by the purest of ears, ears that are themselves of God. (Though this be perhaps a fourth point – that only those ears, those instruments, those hearts and souls blessed by God, may hear His holy voice – we shall incorporate it here; for that which is spoken and that which hears are as one, are so united as to be inseparable in His kingdom, in His realm. And as in the voice there is no noise, so in the ear none is known.)

Before the Blessed Sacrament. Before the Blessed Sacrament exposed to all eyes and all ears, now I write (here at Little Portion Hermitage in the Octave of Easter). Listen for Him speaking here in the silence, alone. Hear His voice radiate here in this sacred space, here in the blessed Presence of God. It sings. It dances. The voice of God is heard clearly, for there is no noise to distract the soul.

There is a fountain of water dripping, very lightly, and this carries His voice, for our ears are open to hear Him – our hearts are centered on His love; dwelling with Him at our center, all is touched by His grace.

Shshsh... no noise. Sing, yes. Shout, yes – but no noise. In Him all is whole. All remains enrobed in silence, this pure silence.

- II -

Then what *is* this silence? If not the darkness of death or the absence of sound, then what? When this silent voice speaks, how do we hear it? How do we know it? How can we speak a name which has no sounds as we know them, yet is itself the alpha and the omega of all sound, and which alone articulates all that is spoken, all that is understood – all that has meaning? He Himself is so far above and beyond our comprehension... yet He has given us His NAME. And this silent Word can be spoken, is spoken in every breath we take in purity.

"YHWH"

Here are the letters. Here is the Word. Here is that which the tongue can make to call upon His presence, in silence.

I. YHWH: The Divine NAME

1.

There are letters.

 Having given us His NAME, He has given us a way to approach Him, to come to know Him – and to recognize when we are in His presence. These letters signify and confirm His presence; they lead us to Him and let us know we are with Him. For the enunciation they represent, the articulation of lips and mouth and tongue they demand, lead us into His silent presence by making still the tongue, the speaking apparatus, and causing us to listen for His voice…
 Yes, the "Y" opens the mouth, poising the tongue for speaking; but before a sound is uttered, the "H" opens the throat, depresses the tongue… and the head is lifted in wonder as light (the light of the Spirit, pure breath) enters the skull. Then as the lips begin to move toward one another ("W"), as if to question this marvel… sound is prevented once more by the opening of the throat again in the final "H". And in this inhalation of light and expiration of any question, of any doubt or darkness, we know His sacred presence.
 He has given us this Word, His NAME for all generations (made flesh in the Person of Christ), that we might indeed approach, that we might indeed know Him – and that we may speak of Him to others.
 What grace the Lord dispenses, letting us come to Him even by human means.

2.

The Word is a paradox.

 The Word, His NAME, is a paradox because though pronounceable, it is silent, and though still, it is yet a spoken word. It is pronounceable silence; it is the moving stillness. As said, it stills the tongue – in its enunciation it halts enunciation – and so it is a word which leads to silence.

It is something of a paradox, too, because all our words (not of noise) are founded in this silence; whatever is truly spoken comes from this silence. God's NAME, indeed God Himself, is the stone on which the temple is built; or perhaps better yet, the temple into which the stones – the stones of our works – are built. The Word (and, of course, the Word made flesh) is the cornerstone of the Church, of the temple we are and we build in His NAME: all is founded on this Word, as all words are founded in His silence. But more to the point, He is the Temple itself and we but mere stones. He is whole, He is all, and we are fitted into Him as pieces.

And we know that one stone shall not be left upon another; nothing of our human hands shall stand on His day. The most beautiful of songs, indeed even Scripture and the Eucharist (as the law was fulfilled with the coming of Christ and the manna stopped when the Israelites entered the Promised Land...), will no longer be necessary in heaven, where we shall know Him as He is – His NAME written upon our hearts – and stand forever in His eternal light. So let us not be distracted by the gleam of the stones, of our works, of our words... Indeed, we have thus a place to burn incense to our God, but let us never lose sight of the foundation and of the Temple itself let us remember always His holy silence. His silence animates all our words: He is the Animator of all we do.

3.

The Word is the Alpha and the Omega.

(Still in the chapel I write, before Jesus, before the Blessed Sacrament... Yes, Jesus is God, is the Word made flesh, and in this way He remains with us, He speaks to us. Here, too, we have paradox, for here is His invisible presence made real to us, calling us to live not amongst the dry bones of a desolate land, but in His Spirit and life...)

I. YHWH: The Divine NAME

Yes, the Lord is the Alpha and the Omega of Scripture (as of all time and space). God, the Word, the silent NAME, the breath which passes through every living creature (YHWH), is at the heart of the Bible, is its very essence. The Bible is an inspired work, not with man or his imagination or the testimony of others as its source, but God – unlike any other work. And its fulfillment, its final form, its effect, is in God's hands as well. Scripture is but one Word spoken by the mouth of God.

And all words are spoken. The spoken word is closest to the source, not the written, for the written word derives from the spoken as a newspaper account derives from testimony of eyewitnesses. And in the end the word on the page is dead, is worthless until read, until *spoken* (to oneself, a neighbor, or a million people). And even the form of spoken words is meaningless if one knows not the language – it is God who communicates through the Spirit. And in His silence comes this communication, at the heart and as the fulfillment of all words. Nothing has meaning apart from Him, for He is all in all, He is life and light… and this Life is spoken in His Word.

Listen to the heart of all words, and you will hear Him speak. Proclaim your words in this silent Spirit of Truth, and Him you will know. As the source and in flesh and bone He dwells. Alleluia.

Footnote

Speaking the letters is not of necessity.

Though speaking the letters of His NAME may aid us in attaining to His presence, in coming into the silence in which we know Him, this means provided is certainly not the sole path to being with Him. But once in His Presence, the Word is upon us.

The Lord may draw us into His presence, into His silence – into His NAME – at any moment and by any means He may choose. And indeed His silence is always with us, within us, in some measure (though indeed He cannot be measured). The manner in which He brings His silence to the fore and makes His light clearly present to us is entirely in His hands. Though His NAME has been given us by

4. YHWH: "Remember My NAME"

Him that we might know Him even in these earthen vessels, God is certainly not bound by this means alone.

And indeed some may become too caught up in the letters, in our speaking of this Word, and fail thereby to fly unto the heaven which transcends it. It is not the letters and the speaking that matter, but the Lord and the coming into His presence. But here we have confirmation of His silent Presence. Here we have the Lord reaching down and drawing us unto Him by means at our disposal. Yes, as Christ has become flesh to draw us unto the Father, so this Word meets us where we are to bring us to where He Is.

Finally, I will say the speaking of the Word, the entering into His NAME, His silence, is extraordinarily simple. It is beyond words to explicate, but it is not in the least complicated. The absolutely simplest matter taking the perfectly least amount of time, it is but to open one's mouth and be quiet.

> "Open wide your mouth and I will fill it."
> Ps.81:11

>One short note, not made elsewhere, regarding the pronunciation of the NAME: a key may be the avoidance of vowel sounds. No "ah" or "uh" should enter in (except to be drawn back from), for it is in uttering these sounds that the silence is broken... But above all, always remain humble, simple – childlike – in speaking God's NAME.

I. YHWH: The Divine NAME

5.

On Speaking the NAME: A Caveat

Speaking the NAME of God, coming into His Presence, opening oneself entirely to the working of the Spirit upon one's soul, although to be done simply, as a child, is not a thing to be taken lightly; for in so doing one indeed opens oneself to the spiritual realm, to the transcendent reality; and losing thereby the walls of earthly rationale, one loses also the benefit of their protection against wandering into lands more suited to the angels. In other words, opening oneself entirely to God also opens oneself to the possibility, if one is not on guard, of the entering in of the devil and his minions – who are spirit as is our God. The devil can tempt the soul in this state with thoughts and inspirations which present themselves as holy, as good, but which are of sin and sensuality. One must be well able to discern sin from virtue, or the soul open to the Spirit's working may be convinced that particularly whatever pet sin it may possess is justified by the Spirit. This is the danger. If I am prone to overeating or drinking, for instance, the pleasure of these activities may take the place of the pure joy of the soul before God, thus dispossessing it from its rightful place and substituting that which is base. Though this is always a danger in the spiritual life, it is particularly so when attaining to such heights of pure worship of God. Thus one must know the sin to which one is prone and be on guard against falling into it, calling it always what it is, and seeking only the purity of God's presence in all humility and wonder.

It should also be noted that just as it is possible for the weak soul to be distracted from pure worship of the Lord, so it is impossible for the corrupted soul to enter there at all. One must be in a state of grace. (And so, let us avail ourselves of regular Confession, and qualified spiritual direction.)

II

Toward an Order

1. *I Am…*
2. Hermit in the City
3. "You Are My Tabernacle"
4. Order of the Divine NAME
   (with Horarium)

NOTE:
The word "order" does not necessarily refer to an ecclesial institution (though if this were the Lord's will, I would not stand in the way). The primary concern here is the ordering of one's spiritual life.

II. Toward an Order

> **"The soul united to God and transformed in Him
> draws from within God a divine breath,
> much like the most high God Himself.
> And God, abiding in the soul,
> breathes forth the life of the soul
> as its exemplar."**
>
> St. John of the Cross
> (from *The Spiritual Canticle*,
> as quoted in Office of Readings for Fri. of the 18th Week in Ord. Time)

– An Introduction –
"One Thing Is Needful"

Mary sits at the feet of the Lord, listening to Him speak, dying to self, to all else, but the Word of God.

We know He will take care of all things
if we trust ourselves to Him.

In Luke 10, Mary gives up her life, symbolized in the hospitality she sacrifices performing in order to be with Jesus. Does she fail to fulfill this blessed duty (so treasured by every Jew) out of laziness, or of neglect? No, she does it for God. And will the Lord leave any good deed required of us undone if we give our lives over to Him? Never. We can imagine that after teaching Martha of the necessity of being present to God and listening to His voice, after having her sit at His feet to find her place with Him, Jesus instructs Mary to help Martha with the tasks of serving, if not joining in Himself.

We think so many things are important, and find ourselves so distracted when we come to pray. But if we give all things else over to the Lord, if we sit silently at His feet listening to His voice – we can be sure He will take care better than we ever could of *any* matter which might distract us from Him

One thing is needful. Come sit at His feet and pray, and listen for His voice.

Peace of Christ!

Herein I present writings toward a spiritual life
founded on the Divine NAME.

II. Toward an Order

    Jesus calls us to take up our cross.
    Jesus calls us to lay down our lives.
    He tells us to renounce all our possessions,
        or we cannot be His disciples.

    But how do we do this? Where do we begin?

    We do this in prayer; this is where we must always begin.
    And here is the very essence of prayer, God's NAME (YHWH),
        and the speaking of His NAME…
        being in His Presence.

    A religious may give up all his possessions,
        he may very well own nothing at all,
        but if his heart is not set on the Lord,
        if he is not in prayer,
        it is all quite worthless.

    Poverty is a means to an end, not an end in itself –
        the end, the purpose, is always union with God.
    And this is always found in prayer; and this is known most fully
        in speaking His NAME,
        for then we give ourselves to Him.

    It is true we must act in His Name, we must do…
        but the first act is always prayer;
        and the rest will follow if first and always
        we remember His NAME,
        if first and always
        we give ourselves to Him –
        if first and always,
        we pray.

1.

I Am...

© *1995*

James H. Kurt

II. Toward an Order

... a mystical poet and philosopher, living, as it were, the life of a monk, whose purpose is to serve as the hub of the wheel, the still point upon which the world turns, hidden and secret, and yet without which the wheel would spin out of place.

The life of the monk is the life of prayer. Prayer, the work of the spirit, is that which sustains life. It is the air we breathe. And though it is invisible, though it cannot be grasped by the hand of man, it serves as life's very essence.

And the word is the tool of prayer, the tool of the monk, the poet, the mystic philosopher. And the word is of God, who is the Word, the Spirit, the source of all life, and all words. With the word the poet speaks, and forms the heart of the universe, the central axis upon which the world spins.

So, though often overlooked and, when viewed, seen as insignificant, if not worthless, the function of the monk is indispensable; it is absolutely integral to the continuation of life, to existence itself.

1. I Am…

As…

…the dirt on the ground,
    the dust of the earth,
is how the poet serves;
    the habit of the monk
        upon his frame,
the mystic is rooted to this plane.

And it is thus his spirit soars,
    it is by this he is set free
to walk in emerald fields…
    For the deeper he enters
        into humility,
the higher he flies
    above the raging sea.

The peace and true solitude
    possessed by this thinker,
which set his soul
    so far apart
from the world's conditions,
are founded firmly upon the rock
    of his demeaning poverty.

II. Toward an Order

Nothing have we.
Nothing are we.

We are nothing, nothing but dust.
From the dust of the earth
the Lord has formed us;
from the clay of the ground
the Lord has made our flesh.
And the black-brown earth is all we are,
is all we could have hoped to be.

Any life in us, any more we are
than this,
comes only by the grace
of the Lord's majesty
and the blessing of His Holy Spirit.

And so does the Spirit bless us,
even as we recognize our sin:
the more we see
that we are nothing,
the greater He enables us
to become...
and so is the least made the first.

1. I Am...

Yes, with nothing we have plenty.
Though alone, we are surrounded
by a cloud of witnesses.
Amid great suffering,
we find joy.

For our refuge is the Lord;
our home is with Him.
And through all manner of deprivation,
we take our nourishment
at His hands.

And so the monk toils in humiliation,
but there finds his peace.
And so the poet speaks alone his verse,
but has the company of Christ.
And so the mystic steps out of this world,
and into the light of God.

Though the fruit of his labor is often unseen,
though quietly and without recognition
he struggles each day –
his work is never in vain...
for it comes to fruition upon the heavenly plane.

II. Toward an Order

Quietly.
Yes, in silence he toils –
*   he speaks in the silence of his heart.*
And though no word is heard
*   by the ears of men,*
*   no sound is hidden from God.*

And so this silent speaking
*   at the center of the universe,*
*   though unknown by the ears of humans,*
resounds clearly in the kingdom of God.

For such is the nature of prayer;
*   this is the work of the Word –*
*   that as we retreat to our closets,*
*   as we plumb the depths of our souls...*
* as we leave behind the things of this world,*
*   we come that much closer to God.*

True prayer speaks the heart of man,
*   speaks the heart of the universe.*
* It is from here all good works come;*
*   this is the place the kingdom rises –*
for, when true, there is God in our soul.

1. I Am...

O God.
O my Lord and King.
O Truth that speaks at the heart of me...

What more could I ask for
   than to be blessed by your love?
What more could I ask for
   than to be filled by your Spirit?
What more could I seek
   than to be the instrument of your peace?

To sit and breathe
   in your light and peace,
 and then to speak
   your truth in poverty...
this is the call of my life;
this is the Lord's purpose
   for all His prophets,
    His poets, priests, and mystics.

And so does the monk exist
   upon this plane:
to bring the blessed peace of God's holy kingdom
to this land in which we dwell.

II. Toward an Order

Even...

...now while I breathe,
 even here where I stand...

the light of the Lord passes through me;
 the Spirit of God is upon me.

Wherever the true mystic may go,
  the peace of the Lord goes with him.
Whenever the poet may live,
  the word of God remains.

Not by time and not by place
  can the truth of God be limited;
to the ends of the earth
   and all through the ages
is present the love of our Lord.

Carry the light wherever you go,
   hold it close
     all the days of your life –
and the Lord shall leave you no more.

1. I Am...

Yes, the light of the Lord
    shall shine forever
      in the hearts of His holy ones;
the love of the Lord
    shall dwell eternally
    now as in the world to come.

Oh, even as the monk speaks,
    even as the mystic breathes,
      even as the poet pens his lines
        of love upon the page...
even now the Spirit lives
    upon the face of this earth.

The Lord shall always leave a light
    to shine amongst His people;
He shall never leave them empty,
    without a shepherd to guide them.

Listen to the monk intone his holy song;
    listen to the mystic reveal the sacred truth;
      listen to the poet unveil inspired words...
and hear the blessed call of the Lord.

II. Toward an Order

The prophets and the saints of old
   who turned their souls to His call
      held the presence of the Lord
in their very heart's core.

And the saints who live today
   are much the same as yesterday;
      for the Lord is not subject to change,
nor then are His holy disciples.

And wherever it is they may be,
   in dungeons or on beaches,
      or walking city streets...
      the Lord of all they carry with them
in the recesses of their souls.

Breathe in the Holy Spirit.
   Live in the Lord's true light.
   The Spirit of God is upon us;
      the kingdom of heaven is at hand.

And it is only the great I AM
   who grants the life of His Spirit
to those who follow His call.

1. I Am...

Be as the mystic who beholds the Lord;
*   live as the monk who heeds His call;*
*   speak as the poet who conveys His word...*
and you shall know the life of the Lord.

At the center of time is an easy stillness
*   and a quiet,*
*   like the eye of a cyclone –*
there you will find the Spirit breathe.

There at the heart of the universe
*   you will come intimately to know*
*   the blessed soul of the Lord.*
And should Jesus come to you,
*   you will be wandering no more.*

Follow Him to the heart of space,
*   to the place where only He dwells.*
Be with Him who is in every land
*   and you shall never be lonely again.*

Cleave to Him and yield to Him;
*   give your very life to Him*
and you shall behold the Son of Man.

II. Toward an Order

Take off your shoes
   for this is holy ground:
 the Lord is here.

Here in the silence,
   the Lord will speak His NAME.
 Here in humility,
   you shall understand His call.

Here where you are even now –
   the Lord is there with you.
 Now at this time,
    Jesus is present.

Everywhere and at all times,
   you may know the voice of the Lord.
 Everywhere and at all times,
   you may dwell in His light.

Always and forever
      and to the ends of the earth,
    the Lord is –
and to come to know Him in all His glory
   you need only open your heart to His Word.

We...

...may be as His prophets:
there is a monk dwelling
in each of us.

In our souls a poet always speaks.
Our spirits have the potential
of the mystic.

God we may touch
at any time of our lives...
The Lord He is always calling us,
speaking to us,
breathing with us
in His Holy Spirit.

Do you not know this?
Do you not know the call of the Lord,
the Word of the Lord
speaking in all things?
Is there no sense of the eternal in you?
Have you not life? Have you not hope?
Does no love abide in you?

II. Toward an Order

Open your mouth and speak with the Lord.
    Breathe with the Lord.
  Take hold of His hand
    and let Him lead you forth.
Allow yourself to become the instrument
    of His grace.

We are all one.
  All are the same person in Christ.
Blessed by His Spirit,
    the sinews of His Mystical Body
      are wrought together.

God has made you a living soul.
God has made me a living soul.
  We are a reflection of His glory.
 There is no separating what God has joined
      together...
  Let us be one in the Spirit.

Accepting the call of the Lord,
  hearing and heeding His voice...
we become His disciples of light.

1. I Am...

We are.
Certainly, we are.

We are one with the Lord of the universe,
  one with Him who is
    the Alpha and the Omega,
    the Lamb of God...
    the Great I AM.

Our souls are wrought inextricably
  into His Spirit,
  into His Life,
  into His Sacred Heart.

I am one with you; you are one with me –
  together we are His holy children,
    radiating His light.

All life comes from Christ.
All light comes from Christ.
All that is good in our existence
  is the product of His sacrifice.

Let us be as He was, as He is.

II. Toward an Order

The poet and the preacher,
* the heart that beats*
*   deep within ourselves...*
the mystic and the monk,
* the soul that breathes*
*   and is ourselves...*

This is what we are.
* This is what we long to be.*
For to be as we are
* is all the Lord*
*   requires us to be.*
And our only wish is to please Him.

He has made us so.
He has formed us in His image;
*   He has shaped us by His love.*
* And so no more does the Lord demand*
*   than we live accordingly.*

To follow the Word
* He has planted in our souls*
*   is simply all that we must do.*
In this all homage is given;
* by this are we made whole.*

1. I Am…

I am so happy
  to be blessed by the Lord.
We are so fortunate
  to have Him as our God.

In these mystical ways
  we come to know His holy presence.
By His sacred hands
  we are made aware.

His children are we:
  His disciples of light.
We speak for Him,
  we live for Him…
  we breathe our very breath for His glory.

Yes, at the center of the universe
  sit His holy disciples.
As the hub of the wheel,
  the world rests upon them.

And our prayers rise as holy offerings;
  our hearts seek His sacred light.
And so we are blessed, and do give blessing.

II. Toward an Order

Are...

...you prepared to be His child?
Are you ready to shine His light?

Are you able to walk in His footsteps,
   in the footsteps that lead to life?
Are your shoulders braced
   for His Cross?

Is the breath that is in you
   relegated to His will –
is it inspired by His grace?
Are there no doubts
   remaining there,
no dark spots upon its purity?

Let the light that is within you
   be not of darkness...
Hide not your lamp's incandescence.

Be as a child of light.
   Burn with mystical fire.
And bring light to this universe.

1. I Am...

Here we are
   as we pray
and offer our lives to the Lord.

In this place we sit,
   or kneel or lie,
ever standing in His grace.

In this place we are,
   there is no turning back,
   no returning to what is past.
All that exists
   is what is present
   in our hearts of light.

Praise the Lord. Sing to the Lord.
   Call upon the Lord
   in truth and in light.
   Make melody to His NAME –
     be filled and shine so bright...

For here in your hearts
   His joy is becoming complete,
   His kingdom is drawing nigh.

II. Toward an Order

And so, ready must we be.
Even now we must be living
   in His own pure light.
  Setting our minds on things that are above,
   our lives must be conformed
    to His will.

No distractions must be allowed
   to enter in.
No confusion, known by the proud,
   must affect our souls.
Only simple, only pure, only humble
   and forgiving
    must we ever be...

For though upon this corrupted plane,
  our eyes must never shine
    with its light.

Only the light of the Lord must fill us.
  Only His holy fire will make us pure.
  Only by His grace will we be ready,
   will we come to know
    His embrace secure.

1. I Am…

Are we indeed ready?
    Do we indeed seek His will?
    Do we hold the soul of the poet?
        Do we possess the cross of the monk?
Does the mystical fire of the Spirit
    of our Lord Jesus Christ
    touch our lives and make us whole?
        Are we as His sons?

The soul of the poet speaks and breathes
    His light.
The cross of the monk humbles all
    our lives.
The fire of the mystic will make us sacred,
    will purge our very hearts
        and souls.

And so by these we will be alive –
    we will come to dwell in the house
        of the Lord
        forever.
No further need have we
    in this present age
    than to sit at the feet of Christ.

II. Toward an Order

Yes, this is the center of the universe:
the feet of the Son of God.
This is where the poet sits.
This is where the monk does kneel.
This is where the mystic rests
and finds his holy vision.

The place where Jesus speaks and teaches
the disciples that come to Him
is where the Spirit breathes –
and so it is indeed the center
of the universe,
for all revolves around His lesson.

So, we must all reside there,
if we are to be ready.
We must take in His light,
take in His words,
take in His guidance
and direction;
if we are to find the way,
if we are to find the truth,
if we are to find the life
that awaits us.

1. I Am...

Now...

...is all that matters.
This is all that will set us free...
   To live the life of God
   is all we really need.

The life of the great I AM
     is present,
       present in all things...
And God is what God will be.

And so we never know,
   nor can we control
      the mind of God;
the Spirit that breathes life
      forth
   surrounds us always
and calls us into His sacred presence
   now, and forever...
And only if we yield to Him
   will we begin to sense –
the eternal wellspring
   that ever begins anew.

II. Toward an Order

Yes, we must abide in the moment,
    for the kingdom of heaven is at hand.
We must accept the Spirit as He breathes,
    and not think beforehand what to speak.

Trust in God,
   understanding of His will,
     is near unto us –
  it is even at the door.

The mystic carries in his heart
   a light that ever shines –
  and it is the light of Jesus.

The poet partakes continually
   of the holy food
held forth by the Hand of God.

The monk remains always
   at the beck and call
   of our holy Lord.

  And each serves the great I AM.

1. I Am…

Now, at this time,
   here, in this place…
  in the midst of us shines
   the eternal light of God's glory –
 and should we but open our eyes,
   we would see it.

The prophet speaks of the coming kingdom;
  as the world rolls on,
  he calls to our conscience:
Seek ye the kingdom of God.
Return, you strayed sheep,
  to His presence.

For upon us now is the destruction of this age.
  Upon us is the end of all things.
 And he who sits at the center of time
   sees this coming,
  and calls to us to change our ways.

The glory of the Lord shines all about us.
   His children are bathed in its light…
  Now is its appointed time.

II. Toward an Order

So, turn not away from His presence;
    delay not to come to His pool –
and refresh yourself with His cool waters…
    redeem yourself in His precious blood.

Come now to receive His special graces.
    Call now upon His holy NAME.
Breathe as one with the Holy Spirit,
    and your life will be renewed again.

The hub of the wheel remains unaffected
    by the turmoil round about its place.
The heart of the saint finds composure
    despite the evil which lies in wait.

There is no greater call
    than the word spoken in truth and peace.
This voice which is of the Lord
    tells us of His vision complete.

And our eyes indeed being open, we see it;
    our ears being clear, we hear.
Washed clean, we find our souls once more.

1. I Am…

We are as He is.
He is, and we are like Him.

The great I AM speaks
   and we listen –
we act according to His Word.

And here at the center of the universe,
   now, as He speaks to us...
  there is no further need to fear;
    no question can perturb our hearts.

For we are: this and nothing more.
  We are alive, we are in His Spirit –
and there is no more we need to know:
   the simple truth of His presence fills us.

So, be as the monk who carries
   the Cross of Christ
   and is set free;
be as the mystical poet and philosopher
who lives and breathes with the holy One –
   and find the life of peace.

II. Toward an Order

an epilogue

The Cross here already
makes real the NAME.

And the Cross is Jesus' Cross;
it is He who carries it...
and so, light indeed it is,
for there is no weight
upon our shoulders.

And indeed there is no weight
upon Jesus,
for He has already died –
the sacrifice has been made
for our sins
and we must but accept it.

So in the Cross is already
the resurrection,
is a peace which surpasses
understanding...
is the NAME of God spoken
clearly to our souls.

2.

Hermit in the City

(explicating a call)

© 2004
James H. Kurt

II. Toward an Order

**"Let us take refuge from this world.
You can do this in spirit,
even if you are kept here in the body."
You can at the same time be here and present to the Lord."**

St. Ambrose, from *Flight from the World*
(as taken from Office of Readings for Sat. of the 2nd Wk. of Lent)

Hermit in the City

The city is a wilderness. A moral wilderness. A wilderness not of trees or wild beasts or desert sands, but of steel and glass and concrete, rife with vice, void of morality. In this barren place I make my home, I pitch my tent, for as long as I must be here on earth.

But, of course, my home is not here at all – the home of every hermit is heaven... for he is far removed from all that surrounds him. So, what is the city to the hermit, what is his wilderness but a place to refine his soul for the gates awaiting all?

And the true hermitage is within. The kingdom in which we long to dwell is now present inside each soul, for it alone animates our being: only the Spirit is alive. What will become known to our human eyes in the day of fulfillment is now ours by faith in Christ dwelling at our very core. So even in this city we cry out, "Abba! Father!" to Him who leaves us not alone.

Enter deeply into that City where the Spirit makes His home: make this Spirit your own. And the distractions around you in this barren land will take no precedence, will have no prominence... will be as if they are not at all. For truly all that matters is heaven – the rest is passing away.

II. Toward an Order

The time is upon us, brothers and sisters. The time is close at hand. Let him who is married live as though without a spouse, him who buys and sells as if he had nothing in his hands – mourn and rejoice, but know neither shall last. The world is passing away.

The end is always near. Always we carry the crucifixion of Christ in our very bodies. Always His resurrection spurs us on to lay down this fading life. There alone light does shine. Whatever light we have here changes soon to darkness.

But by the darkness we are purged. Think not it futile to continue in this land of sunrise and sunset. This time is most valuable to all whose hearts are set on heaven. Here there is sweet preparation – the Cross is not a vain symbol. The blood of Christ cleanses well, that our eyes might open to God's light. Waste not a day, an hour in this wilderness. For the Lord is present to us; His grace in Sacrament we share.

Wonderful Madness!

O the wonderful madness of our Savior!
who cares not for feeding Himself
but only for feeding us
with His presence...

He who takes upon Himself
the guilt of our sins,
who comes from perfection
to dwell with corruption –
and for what?

That He might selflessly offer His life
for an ungrateful lot
such as we are.

What madness is here!
That a man should starve Himself
that others might eat,
and eat a food that shall not pass,
that remains unto eternity...

Without this food I would be dead,
and so I thank you, Lord,
who have died
that I might be nourished
by your sacred Body
and your Blood.

II. Toward an Order

Order of the Divine NAME

For whom is this order founded?
Who is the hermit welcome in its gates?
For whom is this structure built?

For all. For all children of light – of every age, nation, or state... children, adults, single, married, priests, religious... All have His NAME speaking in them. None alive is apart from Him. And so His Breath may be cherished by all.

What of the married, you say, whose concentration is so much on these passing things, whose obligation is to toil and feed? Let your marriage be consecrated to God, to Him who holds all things in His hands. While promising to love, honor, and obey one another, profess first love of God and service of neighbor, knowing that keeping God first and placing others before yourselves, the Lord will bless you and make you fruitful. Think of Paul's words (see 1Cor.7:29-31) – whether you are married or doing business or mourning or rejoicing, do all as if you were not. All is passing. All is passing. Set not your heart on the things around you, on the flesh and on the world. Entrust yourself to the Lord: in His NAME alone will you find peace, will you fulfill any obligation well.

His silence is speaking to all, whoever you are, wherever you are, whatever you must do... Do all with God and not apart from Him and your own soul and spirit.

Father, Son, and Holy Spirit
with the Blessed Mother

This order is Christian, this order is Catholic, and so it is certainly and expressly Trinitarian. All is offered to the Father, the Son, and the Holy Spirit –

> The Father, whose divine mystical wonder,
> whose ineffable Presence we first worship
> (upon whose NAME the order is therefore set)...
>
> The Son, the flesh of Christ and His Cross,
> without whom the Word would be empty,
> without whom we would be as breath without a body
> (we are human beings, not angels,
> and so our faith must be incarnate as Christ)...
>
> The Holy Spirit, the Breath of God Himself,
> speaking to our hearts,
> without whose teaching through Mother Church
> we would soon wander from the true path...
>
> And as for Mary, our Blessed Mother,
>   Virgin Daughter of the Father,
>   Spouse of the Spirit,
>   Mother of the Son...
> How can our faith be pure
>   except that we come through her
>   through whom God Himself has come?

II. Toward an Order

Order

Our first call is to prayer,
and our first work is love:
we must pray at all times
(in the presence of the Lord),
and we must love everyone.

"You have drawn near to Mount Zion and the city of the living God

...only what is unshaken may remain."
(Heb.12:22...27)

And the only way we remain unshaken, the only means to coming to where the Blessed Mother and the saints and angels dwell with our holy Lord, is by remaining in prayer, by remembering God's NAME.

–>

2. Hermit in the City

"No one has greater love
than the man who lays down his life for his friends" (Jn.15:13).

and

"As Christ laid down His life for us,
so we in our turn ought to lay down our lives for our brothers."
We should indeed "love one another as Christ also loved us
and gave Himself up for us."
(St. Augustine on John, see Office of Readings for Wed. of Holy Week)

So, love is our first work and our whole work; in it we follow our Lord, who dies that we might live, that we might love – that we might lay down our lives for all, as He has done.

And in your work you must express your love: "Your work is for the Church, which is the Body of Christ. By your diligence show your love for those whom God has given you." Whether you write on tablets of stone or on hearts of flesh, do all for the Lord, and first, love.
(see Office for St. John the Baptist de la Salle feast day, April 7)

Love and prayer and work are one and the same:
our prayer is work done in love.

The Divine NAME

With every breath we breathe not well,
we take the NAME of the Lord in vain.
For in every breath is the death
    and resurrection of our Lord:

He breathes into our nostrils...
    and so we become a living soul.
We breathe out our mouths,
    commending our spirits into His hands...
    and so die to this life
    but to live again.

Do not take the NAME of the Lord in vain;
do not live apart from Him.
Breathe well, in His presence –
His Word is very near.

2. Hermit in the City

Holy Saturday '04

We Are Dead

We who have resolved to follow the Lord are dead. We live no more for ourselves, but only for the will of God. Into His rest we come, He who rested on the seventh day. Laying down our lives, our wills are no longer our own. And so, we are dead.

The Lord, the Lord alone moves us. St. Paul has witnessed that it is no longer he that lives but Christ who lives in him and he in Christ. Where is Paul, then? He is dead. He has died to himself and lives only in his Lord and Savior. Apart from Him, he is nothing.

And so must we be. There is no sense worrying about our lives, how we should mold and shape them – we must abandon ourselves to the Lord, trusting that He will move us. It is He alone who moves us, He alone in whose hand is our very breath... What have we to say of the movement of our days when our hearts beat for Him alone?

Let us lay our bodies in the tomb with our blessed Lord, and we will take our rest with Him who made us; we will be one with Him who saves us, moved by His Spirit alone.

Mother, with you at the foot of the Cross let us remain, in your blessed arms.

II. Toward an Order

Rise, Let Us Leave This Place

Rise, let us leave this place,
leave this place where death does reign.
From the tomb the Savior calls us
to come into His presence.

Death is all around:
there is no escape known to man.
Only through the wounds
in His side and in His hands
will we live again.

His hand takes our own now,
lifting us from the sleep of death.
He wipes the sweat from our brow,
relieving us from toil
on this empty earth.

In Him alone now light does shine;
peace is in His arms,
spread out upon the Cross in time
and carrying us to our eternal home.

Take refuge in His Name.

Come Closer

Come closer to the Lord,
to His love,
to His discipline –
to His presence this day.

Take a step toward daily Mass,
toward hours of prayer,
toward fasting...
and He will increase your resolve,
and so the fruit you bear.

Practice what you can,
knowing the Lord will ever increase
the fruit of the faithful,
will ever provide our daily bread
until we possess
His abundance.

Come closer to the Lord this day.

II. Toward an Order

Take Reasonable Care

The Catechism instructs us to take reasonable care of our bodies (*CCC* #2288); and so we should, and so is wise. Do not forsake proper service of your body or of your spouse or of your children. For yourself and those in your care you must reasonably provide, for these are of the Lord as are any, as are all. Do not excuse obligations rightly your own.

But do not unduly favor yourself, or your spouse, or God's children in your care. Love them as those of the Lord closest to you, but love all as well – for all who do the will of God are your brother and sister and mother; all are your children... to Christ's Body you are wed.

This takes wisdom to practice well: to love all even as you love yourself. This is your Father's will.

The Body Is Our Hermitage

The body is our hermitage; it is the place we live. This we cannot escape, as we cannot escape the Cross. It is not in rooms we make our home, but in this flesh and in this blood, which we must make our Savior's own.

It is true we worship in a church (and we must), but our temple is always our body. Yes, we live in houses and apartments, cloisters and rectories, but our home is always this frame: it is our cross – we cannot escape it. O let it be glorified!

And the Lord Jesus gives us His own Body and His own Blood to feed us, to give us life, to make our bodies like His own – to assume His glorified form. It is in Him we make our home! Without His sacrifice we would be alone; but as it is, His Sacrament makes us one, and all are in His holy Body... His Blood courses through all our veins. And so the Cross becomes redemptive: it carries us to our heavenly home. And so flesh becomes spirit in the Lord.

The Eucharist Is Ours

The Eucharist is ours, our celebration, our glory, our hope in this world. In the Eucharist we are one, one in the Body of the Lord. In the Eucharist heaven comes to earth. Here we may make our home; here we taste the kingdom.

One in the Spirit, we become one in the flesh, our flesh becoming the Lord's own. Here we commune with the saints, both in heaven and on earth, for here all are one in Jesus. At the Lord's side stands His Mother, and surrounding them are all the saints; the angels sing of our Savior's glory – and through the Eucharist we join in this feast... wed to Him we rise from our knees.

My brothers, my sisters, live in this oneness – live in the kingdom Christ brings into this world. In your heart let the Lord make His home... let His flesh and blood become your own.

In The Father All Are One

In the Father all are one, as in the Spirit and the Son. It makes no difference woman or man, whether you are a priest or a simple workman. All are led to the Father's presence by the only Son of God; and when we arrive in heaven, we shall all see Him eye to eye.

Then there will be no more priests; there will be no more sacrifice... there will be but the One Priest, who offered the One Sacrifice for sin. There will be no need for artisan, for all these things are but the hand of man – in the Father's presence all is done.

Now the Spirit joins us and makes us whole; then what we know now in our soul will be fulfilled in encompassing light... in the kingdom there will no longer be night.

And so no shade will hide God's face, and all the things of this world will pass away. Then we will know what we now understand in our hearts – from the Lord's glory we shall never part.

Each to His Own

To what are you called, my brother, my sister? All are not called to the same place, to the same state. All are called to holiness, yes; all are called to serve the Lord, to bring His Word forth, to reveal His love... but not all in the same way. Let each adhere to his own call.

Are you to marry, and to bear children, populating the earth with holy souls? Then love one another and raise your offspring well – this is your principal call. If to priesthood, then lay down your life for those in your pastoral care. Show them the love of God in all you do and say. And if to religious life God's hand leads you, be prepared to give up all, to love all, to live your life for the Lord alone, and as an offering for all His children.

Each must go to his own call, but each must indeed live for the Lord. And in every soul His NAME must be heard and heeded, for in every soul His NAME does speak, calling all to holiness in Him.

Holiness

"Be holy as I am holy," says the Lord. Be as your God, dear children. To this He calls you in His grace, in His love, in His Son's sacrifice – in His blood. Should you not wash yourselves clean and come before Him... should you not answer such a generous call?

So surpassing is the Father's love for us that He draws us even into His presence, even to be one with Him. What greater love can there be than this, a love embodied, of course, in Jesus the Christ and in His sacrifice? And what greater opportunity could we poor sinners hope for than to be so blessed as to enter that love?

Yet, as surpassing as this call from the Lord may be, still He calls us, still He is defined by such love for His creatures... and He will not cease to draw us unto Himself. Come to Him. Come to His holiness. Be one with the Lord. It is all that matters; it is what is most necessary, and most natural: holiness. Holiness is yours in the risen Lord.

II. Toward an Order

The Lord Is Risen!

The Lord is risen. This is the bottom line, the foundation of our faith and so the heart of any order, of any life lived in Christ. That He is risen from the dead is the indispensable belief we hold to most diligently. Without it our faith would be empty.

And so there is a certain rejoicing, at all times and in all things. Though our life on earth is one of the Cross, though each day we must take up our cross anew and bear it in Christ's name, yet there is joy even in this suffering, for we know it is to God's kingdom we carry our cross. And we know all the while Jesus is there.

He is with us, brothers and sisters. He is alive! No doubt should you have of this simple fact. And so, however alone we may be in this world, however apart from others we may seem, or even physically be, yet we must know, yet we remember – Jesus is always near... and so all His Church lives in our heart.

The hermit indeed lives at the very heart of the Church, not at its outskirts, for in his spirit the Lord is risen, and lives within him on whatever avenue he makes his residence.

2. Hermit in the City
Pentecost '04

<u>In The End</u>
(A logical recounting
of this poetic rendering)

Since this writing has been more of the piecemeal of poetry than of clear delineation – perhaps more evocative than explicative – it would seem wise at the end to draw out the significant points made herein in a more logical fashion:

1) This order is Trinitarian – founded principally on the NAME of the Father and His inexpressible wonder, His surpassing glory to which all are called; its members are united in Jesus the Son and particularly in His sacrifice, shared by all in Holy Mass and in the laying down of our own lives, our sharing in His Cross; and by the Spirit are all souls inspired – whoever we are, wherever we may be... to whatever state we may be called, all are children of our holy Lord, our hearts set on the kingdom above, the kingdom of love.

2) Mary is our Mother, as is the Holy Catholic Church.
And obedience we must give.

3) Our lives are ones of prayer, and the Eucharist is our central prayer, the altar upon which all our prayers, and our lives, are offered.

II. Toward an Order

4) To this order all are called; it is universal as the call to holiness, to being in the presence of the Lord – as any hermit in any wilderness. The kingdom of God is indeed our call, and it is already present within us; give up all of this world (all attachment to anything of this world) to find it.

5) Do not neglect reasonable care of the body, of any in your care, as you draw closer to the surpassing glory of the Lord.

And so, there is little left to say. Commit yourself to the Lord, and He will act. Remember His NAME and that you are in His presence, and He will take care. Love one another with the love of sisters and brothers, and nothing more will you need.

Wherever you are, be with Him.

3.

"You Are My Tabernacle"

© 2005
James H. Kurt

II. Toward an Order

"Do you not know that you are the temple of God, and that the Spirit of God dwells in you?"

1Cor.3:16

– A Preface –

The Finding of Jesus in the Temple

The mystery of the Rosary most characteristic of this order would be the fifth Joyful Mystery, wherein Mary finds Jesus in the Temple that is herself.

Let us consider Jesus' words to His Mother as she kneels before Him in distress expressing her fear at seeming to have lost Him: "Did you not know that I must be in my Father's house?" (Lk.2:49). Does the Child mean to say that He should ever be within these temple walls, these stones raised by human hands? Is He like Samuel, who as a young boy was left in the hands of the temple priests and remained ever there? Or like Joshua, who never left the tent of meeting, the tabernacle of the Lord in the desert? Does He mean to chastise His Mother for not seeking (and leaving) Him in this place?

The only Son would not speak impertinently to His Mother, for He is ever obedient, both to her and to His Father, who demands constant respect for one's father and mother. And He can't be saying that He is to be in this Jewish temple always, for it is so that but a moment later He leaves the temple with His Mother and Joseph (and in less than sixty years this temple will be destroyed).

Yet the Son cannot lie, so when He says He must always be in His Father's house, He means He must always be in His Father's house. Then how is it He keeps His word?

Jesus asks a question of His Mother much like the questions He asks of the Pharisees, and He asks it, as He does all things, with love and compassion. He takes her chin and raises her eyes to His face, and with great sympathy touches her heart with these words... But what does He mean to say? What is it Mary must ponder in her heart?

He means to tell her what every Christian, every human being, should know – that God has created each of us as His holy temple, and she before all others. This is shown by the fact that He leaves the temple with her, that He remains obedient to her – that He remains *ever* with her, as in a temple. And so He does with each of His brothers and sisters and mothers, with all His Church.

II. Toward an Order

Jesus is the Temple of God, His Body the true walls; and though we attempt to destroy this Temple, in three days it is rebuilt… and here we make our home. We are the Body of Jesus Christ. And our Blessed Mother, who is most preeminently the Temple that is His Church, is our way to finding Him and our place in His Body.

The Finding in the Temple (detail)

Mary falls to her knees in tears before Jesus –
the first to find herself there, the first to know His mercy.

She hears His voice. She sees Him teaching. She cries out, "Jesus!" and tries to run to Him, but is blocked by a guard ("That is my Son!" "Woman, how does your concern affect me?"); for He is in a place restricted to men alone. (Indeed, it is only by His grace His Church may enter His presence.) But when she cries His name again, the chief priest cannot but be moved by the piercing tone. He nods his head to the guard to allow her to enter.

She comes in tears on her knees before her Son, so afraid has she been that she had lost Him whom her heart loves. But He touches her face and raises her eyes to His, assuring her He is with her and shall *never* go away. ("Did you not know that I must be in my Father's house?")

She shall never be separated from Him, for she is the House of God, the Temple we all must be. Cleansing us by His grace of all our sins, Jesus dwells within our hearts. Our very bodies are His alone. Yes, we are His tabernacle. Now we enter the holy of holies.

**"In this temple of God, in this Mansion of His,
He and the soul alone have fruition of each other
in the deepest silence."**

St. Teresa of Jesus
(from *Interior Castle*, Seventh Mansions, Ch. III)

"You Are My Tabernacle"

This is the word the Lord gives me at this time. On a morning I enter the chapel and find confusion regarding a misplaced key to the tabernacle; after vain searches and final discovery; as I kneel before the tabernacle, still a little anxious… I hear the Blessed Mother say, "You always have the key to the tabernacle," and then the Lord: "You are my tabernacle." A more wonderful word I could not imagine.

This word is brought to the fore as I read what St. Ambrose says of Jesus' command regarding prayer, *Go into your room* (Mt.6:6):

> But by "room" you must understand, not a room enclosed by walls that imprison your body, but the room that is within you, the room where you hide your thoughts, where you keep your affections. This room of prayer is always with you, wherever you are, and it is always a secret room, where only God can see you.
> (from Office of Readings, Mon. of the 27th Week in Ord. Time)

It reminds me of the hermitage within, wherein every soul makes his home and finds his peace in this world of distraction, a home which every man has at his heart's core. And though the walls of a cloister may certainly assist the soul in finding this place of silence and peace, this place of communion with our Lord in prayer, yet I am reminded also of the quote of St. Francis (whose feast is celebrated this day): "The world is my cloister." The world is our cloister, for all the world is in the hand of God and made as His image, and in every place we must find our home, we must find our peace – we must find the presence of the Lord deep within.

> Note: This work expounds upon eleven "tabernacles" necessary to the spiritual life, to finding union with God… to becoming His tabernacle, a temple of the Holy Spirit.

II. Toward an Order

The Sacrament

Of course, the tabernacle is that which houses Jesus in the Blessed Sacrament, the place He reposes upon this plane. And we who receive Him in the Sacrament, particularly those who receive Him daily, become quite literally His tabernacle, His resting place… the houses where He makes His home. Of this we should be conscious, that we might carry Him with us wherever we go, that we might be true to our call to be His tabernacle.

Thus our bodies truly become our hermitage. Sanctified by Christ in such a real way – presuming one receives in a state of grace, that one as faithfully attends to the Sacrament of Penance – tabernacles of His presence, houses of prayer and worship, do we truly become. And so we realize what St. Paul tells us, that our bodies are temples of the Holy Spirit. And thus are fulfilled Jesus' words to His apostles, His promise that His Father and He would make their home with them, with all who keep His Word (see Jn.14:23). Thus is most wonderfully known the extent of the Lord's great love for His children.

Remain true to the Lord's Sacrament. Do not eat without discerning His Body and His Blood. Do not eat and then quickly forget of what you have partaken; be not like the man who gazes at his image in the mirror and then straightway forgets what he looks like (see Jas.1:23-24). The presence of God comes to us in this Sacrament; the Lord has died that it might be so. And the image of God He would restore in us, if this gift we treasure in our souls.

He is with us always, and makes us one (in Him) with one another. Be holy as He is holy, and eat unto your salvation. Then the presence of Christ you shall see; then His dwelling within you, you shall know. Then the kingdom of heaven will be with you, and your hermitage will be blessed forever. Make your home in the Lord in the body He has given you, by the Body you receive at His altar each day. And His tabernacle you shall be.

3. "You Are My Tabernacle"

Mary

On this feast of Our Lady of the Rosary, it is of course brought to mind that Mary, our Blessed Mother, is certainly the model tabernacle for all the faithful. None is so intimately united with her Son as she who bore Him in her own womb, walked with Him in His ministry, shared deeply in the pain of His crucifixion, and now is one with Him in glory, standing at His side in the kingdom of heaven. Who could be such a tabernacle as she? Who holds Him so perfectly within as does our Lady and our Mother?

Mary is herself the key to the tabernacle of our Lord. Because she is first to know such blessed union with Him, because she is first to confess her faith and accept Him into her very being, it is she we honor above all and are called to imitate. In her wake we indeed follow as we seek the path that leads to oneness with God.

The Ark of the Covenant is Mary the Mother of Jesus the Christ. As she carried Him in her womb, she carries Him still to every soul that seeks to carry Him deep within. As she placed Him in the manger and as she led Him to His sacrificial ministry, so from her place beside His throne she offers Him by the grace of God to all who would receive His presence. He whom she once carried, she yet carries – this is the will of God. For upon His creatures He showers such love… with His creatures He would unite Himself.

Come to Mary and you shall find Jesus. She is the mirror that reflects Him to us; she is the glass that magnifies His presence. If a tabernacle as she you wish to be, if it is your desire to be a true house for our Lord and Savior, then be as your Mother in the faith, and in your soul He will make His home. Then you shall become a temple of the Lord.

Your Church awaits your coming, O Lord. Your Mother leads us to you. Let us be filled with your glory, that we might ever live with you, as she does even now.

II. Toward an Order

The Rosary

And of the Rosary itself a word must be said, for here is the quintessential prayer, which leads the soul so well to mystical union with our Lord and God. Though simple it seem and simple it must be, its depths are beyond our ability to plumb sufficiently. Rarely does the soul enter into that which is presented for our upbuilding, rarely does one partake of the divine nourishment herein, yet eternally is it offered to those of faith who come seeking divine intimacy.

In your hermitage there must be prayer. Your life itself must indeed be lived as a prayer. All your being should proclaim the glory of God. But to find this union with the divine, how shall you begin? To know the Lord and live in the silence of His presence, how can you possibly? His life. It is His life that makes all things possible; His coming amongst us, ministering to us, dying for us, and rising for our sakes, makes available such grace as the soul cannot comprehend. And so, meditation on His life must be your starting point. And what should you say but the words He has given us? And of whom ask assistance but the one the angel declared full of His grace? If you speak with heaven, heaven will be with you; if you have faith in God, His will shall be done.

Raise your heart to the Lord and you will find Him dwelling in your soul. Set your sights upon His life and you shall see your salvation coming. A cloud of peace the Mother shall bring to you if you call upon her blessed name. In this prayer she will lead you to Jesus, who will in stillness make His home with you. A flame in your heart you must have to welcome Him, and to contemplation of His presence you will draw near.

Prayer is all for the soul seeking union with the Lord. In this His love fills us well. Enter the room within you now, and pray with His Mother to know the Lord.

3. "You Are My Tabernacle"

Church Teaching

Do not think the quiet of the inner room can be found apart from Holy Mother Church and obedience to her teaching (as well as participation in her sacraments). If one is not in communion with the teachings of the Church, which are none other than the teachings of Christ, one cannot be at peace, for one will not be living in truth. Try as we might to convince ourselves of some utterance that contradicts the faith and morals of our Mother, we shall come inevitably to a desert place where, if we are blessed, finally realization of our errant ways will be brought up before our eyes. Without trust in her, we have no trust in God, and without trust in God we are certainly lost.

The devil never ceases to whisper in our ears, flattering us with the measure of our intelligence, or of our righteousness before God. He does so that we might presume greater understanding than the ages speak – than the martyrs who have suffered and died, than the Fathers who have sought through all darkness and vanity to discover the light, than the virgins and all the humble souls the Lord has touched with His blessed Hand… yes, even than Christ Himself. What excuses Satan inspires, what empty reasoning he brings to mind to infuse with false light the imaginings of a diseased heart. But God cannot be made to fit our own ideas of what should be (lest we die); rather, we must conform to Him who has made His creatures from the dust of the earth. So, entertain no fleeting thought or pet theory on any matter defined already by your Mother – be obedient instead to her commands, to her words of genuine light and truth, and in her wise counsel you will find your peace.

There is a false compassion afoot, my friends. It enters the heart and makes its home, unbeknownst to the sleeping soul. Those who are not vigilant, who do not question the theories of the age, will not see the ends to which they lead – perhaps until it is too late. Take the word of Mother Church as truth. Even though you may not fully understand it, give it the benefit of acknowledgment as the teaching of Christ, and soon it will prove itself to you; and in it you will find your home.

A tabernacle you cannot become if not in the House of God.

II. Toward an Order

Holy Scripture

And if not rooted in Scripture, how can you hope to hear the Word that is spoken most clearly there? The still, small voice is what inspires every verse of the Holy Writ; the NAME of God is present in every passage… and if you do not read what is contained there, how can you hope to draw close to Him? How can you expect to know His peace and light and become as a child of the Lord Most High?

Holy Scripture is as a mirror, a reflecting pool in which we might see our soul, in which we might find ourselves in conversation with the Lord. Here God speaks to us, if our ears are open to His voice, if our hearts are not closed to His love. Here He speaks and prepares our souls to receive Him well when He comes to us… when He comes to us in His Sacrament, and when He returns at the end of the age. And He cannot make His home with us if we are deaf to His Word. And a tabernacle we will not remain if we do not often visit Him.

Scripture should be our very bread, nourishing every breath we take. It must be the leaven growing ever in us, till we rise to maturity in His presence. The readings of Holy Mass in particular should daily inspire our actions, should be found at work in our lives – in them we have a regular mirror to discover the instruction the Lord imparts. All of Scripture is God's prophecy (and the Gospels, of course, hold special weight). With it as a whole we should be familiar, reading it even cover to cover.

Scripture is indeed one Word. That Word is the NAME of God – YHWH. In silence it is the Lord speaks to us, and there is the most profound silence here at the heart of the Bible. Listen for Him speaking. Come to Him as a child, a child trusting in the Spirit. If the Holy Spirit is not with you as you read its verses, then better to put the book aside, that no false light capture your thinking. But if a tabernacle of the Lord you would be, then come to its pages quite freely, and obediently accept the wisdom given to you, in a spirit of repentance. Though deeper than any ocean are its waters and you shall never fathom all it says, yet little by little you must drink there, that you might build up your spirit, that you might find your house set on rock.

Holy is His Word, and holy are those who hear and keep it.

Liturgy of the Hours

If it is essential to surround one's day with prayer to become a tabernacle of the Lord, then, in addition to wrapping one's soul in the arms of the Blessed Mother by continual recitation of the Holy Rosary, one should practice the great prayer of the Church: the Liturgy of the Hours. Here in these psalms and canticles, here in these antiphons and readings... here in these hours of prayer we find the very beams of the temple we wish to build within ourselves.

Here is another limpid pool wherein we gaze as if into a mirror to see our souls, to read God's Word speaking to us always and revealed in a special way at these five (or seven... or at least two) times a day. Each time we open our breviary the Lord speaks to us, if we listen. And even if our minds are dull, even if our bodies are weak, our eyes closing from the work of the day – even if in a meditative state we do not come to contemplate the Word of God, still its recitation gives us a home... and still a word, if only one, will reach into our souls from upon the page. (Be faithful to prayer, brothers and sisters.)

Here in the psalms – the lion's share of this prayer – we view ourselves as in a mirror, yes; but, more so, we hear the very voice of Christ Himself speaking and Him spoken of: His trials and tribulations, His sufferings and persecutions... and His joy and the glory of His triumph as King of the universe and King of our hearts. Here is the drama of the Son of Man hidden in these verses and making itself known to the watchful eye. It is He who speaks; do listen. It is His life we have – imitate His glorious way of the Cross.

And in here you will find the walls of the tabernacle solidly built. This is a house of prayer for all God's children. By these hours your time will be constructed according to the will of the Father, and His tabernacle He will make you.

II. Toward an Order

Children of Light

Then, we must speak of the innocence of children. "Unless you turn and become like children, you will never enter the kingdom of heaven" (Mt.18:3). If Jesus tells us we must be childlike, how can we ignore His command, except at the risk of our lives? Unless we have that childlike trust and simplicity, the doors of the kingdom will be closed upon us.

For if God is beyond our ability to comprehend, if His peace passes our understanding, how shall we come to Him by the power of our own minds, by the strength of our own wills? All must be given over to the Lord, our vision must be perfectly pure... nothing of this world can hold our attention, if we are to know His grace – if we are to look upon His face.

And such purity only a child possesses. Such freedom to trust, to believe in His goodness, only a child exercises. For the child is humble, silent before the figures hovering over him. The child is innocent, with no devices of his making to corrupt his soul. The child alone gives his life entirely to that which is before him – and that which is before us is always God. (Only a child hears His voice.)

A child holds all the universe in his simple spirit; as the hermit must love all, must pray for everyone – must be concerned that all God's Church is blessed, that all souls enter His kingdom (for none will fully know Him until all are present to Him) – so he must be as a child, for then alone will he find such grace, such blessing from the Father of the heavenly race. To the angels we shall be joined only if our eyes gaze upon them always, only if our own angels behold the face of the Lord at all times.

You cannot be a tabernacle of the Lord if you are not pure, and you will not be pure if not like a child. Mary is pure and so His Tabernacle. The Church is pure and so His Tabernacle. Scripture is pure and so His Tabernacle... And you, son of man, must be pure, innocent as a newborn, filled with the Spirit of God, if you too would hold the Lord within yourself, if you would have Him hold you in His Hand.

3. "You Are My Tabernacle"

Chastity

Chastity is, of course, of utmost importance if one is to become a tabernacle of our Lord, for, again, if the tabernacle is not pure, it certainly is not of the Lord.

Chastity is generally equated with celibacy, with abstention from sexual activity, both internal and external, and, much as cloister walls can serve well the finding of the hermitage within (which is of ultimate consequence to every soul), so can celibacy well serve and in a certain sense perfect the unalterable call to chastity. But it is not in celibacy alone that chastity makes its home, for all souls in whatever state must be chaste, according to the decree of Mother Church. And so the chastity necessary to found one's tabernacle must be known in that state of life to which one is called.

Thus in marriage one must be chaste, as in religious life or single life or ordained ministry one must be chaste, one must be pure. Though it may be a challenge and a struggle for a soul in any state of life, the struggle cannot be abandoned – except if the Lord should take it from us. (It is really He alone who maintains us in our chastity, as in all things.) Always we must strive to be pure of heart, for it is then alone we may see God and know His presence within us.

Our bodies are indeed our temples, our tabernacles – our first cloisters even if we should live out our lives behind walls. If the body is not pure, is not whole, is not chaste in accord with the Lord's command to keep our eye and heart clean… whoever we are and wherever we are, we will not be making our home in the Lord's house.

The saints were greatly celibate. This is understandable. It is in harmony with Paul's recommendations regarding marriage and virginity (see 1Cor.7), and with our Lord's own word concerning becoming a eunuch for the kingdom of heaven (see Mt.19:10-12). But as each also says, this is not for everyone, but only those who are able to heed such a call. But for all, chastity must be maintained to remain in the good graces of God and live as His holy tabernacle.

II. Toward an Order

Poverty and Obedience

Along the same line, poverty and obedience, the other two of the evangelical counsels, must be practiced by all of any state in life.

Perhaps more than any of the three, we relate poverty to the call to religious life, where all is held in common, where no monk or nun, brother or sister, owns anything. And perhaps (though husband and wife are called to share all things as one) because marriage seems so bound up with material things, which are so necessary to raising well a healthy and whole family, it would seem there is not a place for poverty here (or in the single or ordained state), particularly in the age in which we dwell. But all must be bereft of everything to enter the kingdom of heaven.

To be bereft of everything does not necessarily entail selling all one has and giving it to the poor, as do the religious. For what is of significance here – again, as with our cloister analogy – is not so much that we own nothing, but that we possess nothing with our hearts… in a word, that we are *attached* to nothing. It would certainly seem easier to accomplish this call if one is actually in ownership of nothing, as in a religious community; but even in the religious state one must have no *desire* for things, or one's poverty is quite in vain.

And in marriage is one not to be obedient to one's spouse and, even more fundamentally, obedient to God? Does one in a single state – not attached to a religious order, not ordained – have any less obligation to be obedient to Holy Mother Church, as well as all rightful authorities? Certainly all must practice the obedience required of one's state.

Without poverty one does not live with God; one lives with the world. And without obedience one could never trust the house one builds or find any reason to believe he is in communion with the Lord – for He demands obedience before all else. To be God's tabernacle, the evangelical counsels must all find place in you.

3. "You Are My Tabernacle"

The Saints

It is the feast of St. Jude, a popular saint among the people I know. The saint of hopeless causes. Many souls I know are aware of their sinfulness, their hopelessness before God. But we have the saints to help us.

The saints were once as lost as we. (The Blessed Mother is, of course, an exception. The first of saints, she, having been immaculately conceived, is clearly different, placed above all other saints – and even the angels – though more distinctly below the level of God.) They were lost, they were sinners… but now they are saints. And so they are our brothers and sisters.

Now they are in heaven, but once they were on earth – much as the Lord Himself, who, though never a sinner, took upon Himself the sins of mankind. (It is, of course, in the Lord Jesus the saints make their home, by whom and through whom and in whom they are saints at all.)

They who once toiled here where we toil are now safely within the gates of heaven, where neither heat of day nor dark of night can any longer touch their sacred souls. Do we not wish to be where they are, to be as they are… with our Lord Jesus? And will these not help us in Jesus' name?

We are in a communion, brothers and sisters; we are a family. We are not alone. Neither heaven nor earth separate us from the kingdom of God, and all in Christ are one even now. If we isolate ourselves from communion with our brothers and sisters in heaven or on earth, we isolate ourselves from communion with God, who has commanded us to love our neighbor as ourselves – and in such isolation our tabernacle is lost.

Though in the desert we may dwell, yet alive in us must be the Lord; and He is not alive in us if not with others of our kind. We must know our oneness with our brothers, the saints, and find the help the Lord has ordained they offer. Else our cause shall indeed be hopeless… and our tabernacle we shall never find.

II. Toward an Order

Death

Death. Death is the doorway to heaven, our only means to God's kingdom. If we do not die, we shall not live; we shall not be His temples.

It is the Solemnity of All Souls. All souls must indeed be purged; all souls must indeed be emptied of life, the life of this world, to find the life of heaven. Is it painful? Yes. Is it easily desired? No. But it must be done; and our solace is always that by the grace of God our death leads to His kingdom.

But death must begin now, must begin here where we are. On this earth Christ calls us to His Cross, calls us to the laying down of our lives – this is what our existence is all about. If we do not empty ourselves here and now, if, rather, we fill our hearts with the things of the world, how shall we be prepared for heaven? And can we be assured we will even enter there? If we do, it will only be as if through fire.

Do not be afraid. This is what Jesus says; this is what the Lord comes to grant us: His peace, His rest – through His light burden – is ours under the Cross. The more we come to share in His sacrifice, the greater pain we may know, but the greater peace will be ours... because it is His sacrifice we share, and not our own.

Die we must. Empty of all else we need find ourselves, or there will be no place in us to receive God's gracious presence; for He demands all of our souls, all of our wills, all of our very beings – for no less love would He grant to us.

May the Lord make His home in you, even as you die to yourself. Even as you lay down your life in this world, the life of our Savior will be your own.

4.

Order of the Divine NAME

for all Children of Light

Out of Darkness

Chaos is darkness, is lack of order; the Lord gives us a will in union with His own to bring order out of chaos, as He has done. Left to itself, the world, as a spoiled child, would bend toward darkness rather than the light which is its natural home, for the world has been corrupted by sin. By Jesus and His blood we strive to bring light to this forsaken universe, to redeem man from his sinful state.

> This order is Marian, consecrated under the mantle of the Blessed Mother; but first this order is Trinitarian. For from the silent Word (YHWH, God the Father) – the NAME we especially commemorate – all is spoken; and what is spoken, by the power of the Holy Spirit, is Jesus, the Word made flesh, and His Cross.
>
> > Herein I share what progress I have made
> > in finding a spiritual life in God.

II. Toward an Order

Four Principles
of the Order of the Divine NAME

1. **To pray,**
   the silent NAME of the Father written upon our souls.
2. **To pray for the salvation of all souls,**
   the sacrificial blood of Jesus the Son coursing through our veins.
3. **To work,**
   led by the promise of the Holy Spirit and infused with His light.
4. **To work for the upbuilding of the Church,**
   by the intercession of Mary, the Mother of God and of us all.

4. Order of the Divine NAME

– Spiritual Practices Outline –
In Descending Order of Importance
(and Groups of Three)

I. Silence, Speaking the NAME of the Father

A. These practices are never omitted.

1. **Daily Mass**
2. **Weekly Confession**
3. **Daily Plenary Indulgence**

B. These practices are sometimes partially missed but usually made up.

1. **Reading Sacred Scripture**
   (esp. Mass readings)
2. **Liturgy of the Hours**
3. **Full Rosary**

C. These practices are occasionally abridged.

1. **Fasting**
   (bread and water, Wed. & Fri.)
2. **Other Spiritual Reading**
3. **Other Devotional Prayers**

NOTES:

- The essence of prayer, and this order, is silent contemplation
  (speaking the NAME of the Father, YHWH);
  it is listed as a separate practice, and as the first and only,
  because, as I say, it is the quintessence of *all* prayer.

- The grouping (A, B, C) may illustrate levels of commitment
  if an order is to be founded.

  - Also, work is, of course, a part of the discipline,
    as is service to others and tithing...

II. Toward an Order

The Elements of the Building –
(some of which do overlap)

General

Silent Contemplation, eternal

Three Hours of Prayer:
  the First Hour,
    the Last Hour,
      and the Hour of Vigil

Holy Hour(s), daily

A.

Daily Mass

Weekly Confession
(or at least every twenty days,
 to gain plenary indulgences…
 and monthly spiritual direction)

Plenary Indulgence, daily[1]
(esp. Stations of the Cross)

B.

Reading Sacred Scripture
(re the day's Mass,
 and continuous)

Liturgy of the Hours
(five times daily)

Full Rosary, daily
(three to five Mysteries)

C.

Fasting on Bread and Water,
Wednesday and Friday

Reading the Saints' Writings
(and other spiritual reading)

Reading Catholic Periodicals

Consecration to
the Blessed Mother
(St. Louis de Montfort)

Entrustment to
Our Lady of Mt. Carmel,
and Morning Offering

Wearing of Brown Scapular

Wearing of Divine NAME
Scapular[2]

Wearing day's liturgical color[3]
(for shirt; with black pants)

Carrying of Rosary
and St. Benedict's Cross

Prayer of Prostration

Morning Invocation
of God's Blessing

Spiritual Communion prayer
(St. Alphonsus de Liguori)

Prayer before a Crucifix

Anima Christi

Novena to Infant Jesus

Noon Angelus

Divine Mercy Chaplet

Nightly Examination
of Conscience

Work – Daily Bread, as called

Also, Service & Tithing
(e.g. Nursing Home Visits
 & 5% Parish + 5% other…)

4. Order of the Divine NAME

Horarium

"His commandments are not burdensome" (Lk.5:16)
and should not be made so – all practices must lead to recollection.

Sketch:

2:00 – 4:00: Vigil Hour(s)
- Silent Contemplation
  (Speaking the Father's NAME)
- Office of Readings
- Reading of Day's Scripture,
  and Writing…
- Prayer of Prostration

4:00 – 5:00: Rest
(in the Lord's arms)

5:00 – 6:00: First Hour
- Glorious Mysteries, sung
- Invocation Prayer
- Morning Prayer
(and other prayers:
renewal of consecration,
offering to Our Lady…)

6:00 – 7:00: Breakfast,
Dressing, Walking to Church
praying additional Rosary,
meditating on the Church…

7:00 – 9:00:
In Church/Chapel
- Stations of the Cross
  (for plenary indulgence)
- Holy Mass
- Holy Hour before the Sacrament
    Joyful Mysteries
    Spiritual Reading/Writing
(Walk home, Luminous Mysteries…)

9:00+ – 12:00: Work

12:00: Daytime Prayer
with Noon Angelus

12:00+ – 2:00: Dinner,
with newspaper reading, EWTN…

2:00 – 3:00:
Luminous Mysteries,
while walking (if not in a.m.)…
and rest/nap

3:00: Divine Mercy Chaplet

3:00+ – 6:00: Work

6:00 – 7:00:
- Evening Prayer
- Shower
- Evening Collation…

7:00 – 8:00:
Television News

8:00 – 9:00: Last Hour
- Examination of Conscience
- Night Prayer
- Sorrowful Mysteries, breathed

9:00 – 2:00: Sleep

II. Toward an Order

Full Description:

2:00 – 4:00: **Hour of Vigil** - actually, closer to two hours
(generally an hour later for Sundays & Solemnities… making the hour of vigil 3-5)
Silent Contemplation[4], speaking the NAME of God – YHWH (20 min.)
Obviously, since this serves as the charism of the order outlined herein, such silent contemplation is at the heart of the life of the soul for whom these hours are being laid down[6]. Just as obvious should be the fact that such practice is not confined to this short time. Contemplation of God's presence, speaking His NAME – conversation with the Lord and His Mother – should be constant, at the beginning, middle, and end of *all* prayer, and indeed all one's life. One ever returns to it and ever remembers it, ever coming into the Lord's presence… thirsting like Mary to sit at His feet.
Office of Readings (15-20 min…)
Whether chanted in tandem with others, whispered silently or spoken aloud, whether sung in joy or cried in supplication, all hours should be prayed in recollection – to God and with God, in conversation with Him and His Church. (Also, Office reading and prayer (from own book) re the saint of the day.)
Reading of Scripture for the Day's Mass (40 min.+)
(Preceded by review of previous day's readings, and writing of a sentence on them.)
Careful/gradual reading, in the spirit of lectio divina, three times through… Parallels should be discerned, meaning found, which one may afterward write down; this illumination should serve as a catalyst for the prayer of offering following, and such prayer begins even while reading. One might also peruse a commentary on the readings or review other passages from the Bible that might be related… After 2nd time through, I read the exposition of each day's Scripture I've composed in *Our Daily Bread*; after 3rd time, I chant the verse I've composed for each day.
After reading, one should improvise a song of prayer to the Lord reflecting the readings of the day, offering oneself and the Church and world in accord with their message. One may also sing in tongues, as inspired.
(And I've begun a prayer journal to the Lord at this time.)
Prayer of Prostration, offering of one's day (10-15 min…)
On knees, shins flat, forehead bowed to ground (or fully prostrate on face and stomach with legs back, arms forward) and cloth used to cover shoulders during all hours of home prayer covering one's body. One should go through each particular event and action of the day, asking God to bless all one plans to do – i.e. what is outlined in this horarium, and especially that one will bring the Lord's peace to every place one goes and pray for the salvation of all people one meets… thanking Him for all His blessings.

4:00 – 5:00: **Rest**, in the Lord's arms.

4. Order of the Divine NAME

5:00 – 6:00: First Hour
Glorious Mysteries, sung; I have set aside an intention for each decade:
1) Family 2) Friends, Neighbors… 3) the Church 4) one's Country 5) the World as well as for each Hail Mary. (Not prayed Saturday Morning… still in tomb.)
Invocation Prayer[6], meditative (5 min.): dying to sin, living to God.
Morning Prayer (15 min.) and **additional prayers** (5 min.), including St. Louis de Montfort's daily **Renewal of Consecration**[7] to Jesus through Mary and **Morning Offering** to Our Lady of Mt. Carmel.

6:00 – 7:00:
Breakfast, Dressing, Walking to Church praying additional **Rosary**, meditating on the Church from apostolic times to the Second Coming.

7:00 – 9:00: In Church/Chapel
Holy Mass preceded by **Stations of the Cross** (for **Plenary Indulgence**, except Sundays & Solemnities, when Joyful Mysteries serve this purpose; no 15th Station Sat. & Lent) as well as St. Alphonsus' **Prayer for Spiritual Communion**[8] (3x: before Mass, and before & after Communion). After Mass, **Prayer before a Crucifix** and **Anima Christi**.
One should obviously be most recollected – speaking the Lord's NAME, remaining in His presence – during the holy sacrifice of the Mass.
Holy Hour…
(Sacrament exposed, if possible; otherwise, before tabernacle):
   Joyful Mysteries, wherein, along with the mysteries, one meditates on
   A) one's personal annunciation in reception of Communion (seated)
   B) visiting Jesus in the Tabernacle with Mary (kneeling)
   C) giving birth to Jesus, even as our Blessed Mother (head bowed to ground)
   D) offering oneself to God, as Mary offered Jesus (prostrate, arms forward)
   E) becoming as a tabernacle of the Lord, as is our Blessed Mother (sit on heels)
   Followed by **Spiritual Reading**, especially of the **Saints** (John of the Cross, Teresa of Jesus, etc.)**,** the **Bible**… and **Writing**
   (Before leaving church, **Infant Jesus Novena**… to remember the Father's NAME in one's soul, the Son's Blood in one's heart, and the Spirit's Promise in one's mind… one with Mary and the Church in the Body of Christ.
   Walk home praying **Luminous Mysteries**…)

9:00+ – 12:00: Work
For me, especially writing (including typing, proofreading, publishing, recording, podcasting, promoting…); also, errands such as food shopping, laundry, et. al., as well as community service, additional prayer, etc. (Of late I have been making an additional Holy Hour(s) before the exposed Sacrament during the day. I long to have perpetual access to the Sacrament in a House of prayer.)

II. Toward an Order

12:00: **Midday Prayer** with **Noon Angelus** (as opening hymn)
One may need to say Daytime Prayer earlier (Midmorning, say 9:30 -11:30) or later (Midafternoon, say 1:30 – 4:00), depending on schedule, but one of the three Daytime hours should be prayed each day, with attention.

12:00+ – 2:00: **Dinner** (main meal of the day)
Cooking, eating, washing dishes…. with **reading of Catholic periodicals** (National Catholic Register, Our Sunday Visitor…), watching EWTN… Wednesday and Friday one fasts on bread and water at every meal.
(When falling on Wed. or Fri., Solemnities like Sun.; Feasts just no meat.)

2:00 – 3:00:
If not prayed walking home from church in the morning…
Mysteries of Light, while walking through the park;
time for rest and/or work resumes earlier (esp. Wed. & Fri.).

3:00: **Divine Mercy Chaplet**
Before image, on knees (freestanding) with arms out

3:00+ – 6:00: Resumption of **Work**

6:00 – 7:00: Evening Prayer - Shower - Evening Collation…
light meal; meat should be eaten no more than once a day, at dinner time, deserts reserved for Sundays and Solemnities.

7:00 – 8:00: Hour of Television
Quality news rec. (News Hour with Jim Lehrer personal preference) to keep regularly informed of events of the world, to better keep the world in prayer.

8:00 – 9:00: Last Hour
Examination of Conscience
Night Prayer
Sorrowful Mysteries (exc. Sat. & eve of Solemn., in anticipation of resurrection) breathed… a phrase on inhalation, and one on exhalation[9]; often in tears, rosary in left hand, crucifix in right, seated in bed, in darkness…
1) leaning back against headboard, knees somewhat up
2) leaning forward, legs flat, knees out
3) back flat against headboard, legs forward, flat
4) leaning further forward, legs forward and out, flat
5) only head propped up, one knee up, arms out…

9:00 – 2:00: Sleep

4. Order of the Divine NAME

NOTES:

[1] Plenary Indulgence

In keeping with the charism of praying for the salvation of souls, plenary indulgence prayers are of critical importance. (Dispensation may even be sought for multiple daily plenary indulgences: for Stations, Full Rosary, Rosary in church and/or with family, Scripture Reading, etc.).

[2] Divine NAME Scapular

The scapular for this order is an icon of the Trinity. In front is the NAME of the Father (YHWH), for as Jesus says, "The Father is greater than I" (Jn.14:28), and to the Father we have special devotion; on the back is a symbol of the Son and His Cross, of the blood He shed for our salvation – INRI – the Latin acronym for "Jesus of Nazareth King of the Jews", and the sentence for which He merited crucifixion (which was posted above Him); at either shoulder soaring between Father and Son are doves symbolizing the Holy Spirit, who bears God's promise to us... and a pin of Mary praying holds the letters INRI to the back of the shirt, for it is by Mary and by her prayers that we come to Jesus and so to the Trinity.

[3] Liturgical Colors

Option is always for the saint's day, red the preference over white

[4] Silent Contemplation / Speaking God's NAME (YHWH)

Perfect silence should be striven for, but, not feasible to maintain for twenty minutes (since even a constant minute may be difficult to keep – and even a split second is long enough to enter His presence...), other practices will enter, including speaking in tongues, which comes from this divine silence and speaks of it, as well as conversation with the Lord regarding questions of the soul. Ejaculations such as "My Lord and my God," "Come, Holy Spirit," "I Love You, Jesus," and even "Mommy" (when calling upon the Blessed Mother) will also inevitably arise.
Similar to centering prayer, one should use a prayer word, in this case the perfect Word, the NAME of God: breathe in speaking "YH", out speaking "WH"; that is, poising the mouth for speech – wind entering and igniting

II. Toward an Order

fire in the mind (YH); then pursing the lips, offering all one's self up while exhaling (WH)... For breath in, one's head may go back, even to looking straight up, mouth wide open (and may pause there at times, captivated by the light, perhaps in tears, perhaps smiling...); and for breath out, head may go down to even (or at times bowed in utter humility before the Lord's overwhelming presence). Or one may speak the entire NAME – which is the heart of all speech, all human intelligence – in a single moment of calm, childlike illumination (see One Breath note at end). Also, looking upon an image of the printed letters (YHWH) should prove helpful. (Most helpful, of course, is the presence of the Blessed Sacrament, preferably exposed.)

[5] for the Soul...

Though outlined particularly for the life of a hermit/monk, which, though recently married, most closely characterizes my own state, certainly the practices within could be applied by anyone, single or married, priest or mother... There is a hermit in each of us, and to whatever extent one may be called to this spirituality, to whatever extent one's station allows, so are these practices appropriate. And there is, of course, room for variation... Even in my own life there is not a strict adherence to these hours every day. Though all are generally kept, some are more essential than others (see Spiritual Practices), and the discipline is subject to adjustment. But the closer I get to this order, the more perfect I do seem to become.

[6] Morning Invocation Prayer (may be improvised upon)

> Lord, let me be dead to sin:
>   dead to the flesh, dead to lust and sloth and gluttony;
>   dead to the world, dead to anger and greed and envy;
>   dead to the devil, dead to pride.
> Let me be alive, alive in virtue and goodness:
>   alive in the Holy Spirit and His gifts,
>   alive in the kingdom of heaven with your angels and your saints,
>   alive with you, dear Lord, in the glory of God the Father.
>
> Open my nostrils to breathe your Spirit;
>   fill my lungs with your breath, my soul with your peace...
>   let me be one with you in your presence
> Open my ears to hear your voice;
>   let my heart beat in obedience to your word,
>   your blood, your love, coursing through my veins.

4. Order of the Divine NAME

Open my eyes to see your light;
> pierce my mind with your wisdom,
> that I might articulate your will in patience.

.Open my mouth to humbly receive your food;
> strengthen me this day for doing good,
> for accomplishing your work in this world.

O Lord, open my pores to receive your touch;
> let your innocence and purity fill my spirit,
> that I might be a child of your light,
> a branch of your holy vine.

Blessed Mother,
> I entrust myself into your arms, your hands, your heart;
> may I be molded in your womb
> into the image of your Son
> by the power of the Holy Spirit,
> that I might truly be a child of God the Father.

Lord, I thank you for my life this day;
> please bless me, heart, mind, soul, and strength,
> and make my spirit one with your own.
> Remain close by; let me remember your NAME.
> (silence (YHWH); then, rising...) I love you!

[7] St. Louis de Montfort's
Prayer for Daily Renewal of Consecration to Jesus through Mary

> "I am all Thine and all that I have belongs to Thee,
> O my sweet Jesus, through Mary, Thy holy Mother."

[8] St. Alphonsus de Liguori's
Prayer for Spiritual Communion

> "My Jesus,
> I believe that Thou art really present in the Most Holy Sacrament.
> I love Thee, and I desire Thee; come to my soul.
> I embrace Thee; and I beseech Thee
> never to allow me to be separated from Thee again."

II. Toward an Order

[9] On Perfection of Prayer

May also speak a phrase only on exhalation. Here would be employed what I would consider perfect prayer, utilizing heart, mind, soul, and strength to the full. One would be silent upon inhalation, employing the soul by speaking the NAME of God, and employing the mind by imagining the scene proper to the Mystery. Upon exhalation one would employ the body by speaking the words, clearly and unto Heaven (to the Father or to Mary), and at the same time lift one's heart up to the Lord, literally raising the bloodstream in a kind of emotional sacrifice. Praying in this fashion would double the time for the Rosary. This method is especially appropriate for the Sorrowful Mysteries, wherein patience is the great virtue to be sought. It also prepares one well for the death that is sleep.

One Breath: A General Note

We have talked here of the NAME of God as breath, as a breathing in and out in pure spirit... and so as two motions: I have said the first part of the NAME (YH) causes breath to enter, and the second part (WH) to exit – inspiration and expiration, as it were, the constant interplay of life and death (and resurrection) in our lives that keeps us in constant prayer with our Lord and our God, if we set our hearts and minds on His presence breathing in and out of our bodies. (O what a wonder it is to be in continual communication with the Lord in prayer!) But I should note that ultimately the breath of which I speak is one. Ultimately, indeed, there is no breathing at all; there is only light, only the presence of our Lord.

The Logos, the Word, is, of course, not a word at all, but life. And when one enters the presence of God, of Life itself (where is no death), when one comes upon pure being in one's prayer, in one's speaking the NAME of the Lord... there is but stillness there. The tongue is stilled, all breathing stops (or at least becomes inconsequential), and all we know is the light of God. The Word upon us fully, we see that the Word is one and unmoving – all the NAME is spoken simultaneously. Breath in and out become one and the same in the NAME, and God is present in all around. (And I look all around to see Him... Where is He? Everywhere.

Here where the tongue is stilled we must seek to come. (And this can be done, too, by simply opening the mouth and depressing the tongue from the throat – opening the throat for pure breath in this way.) Here where there is no more pride, no more words man would assert in his own name... here in God's Presence let us make our home.

III

Into Practice

1. Sylvia
2. A Third Pilgrimage
3. A Married Hermit

III. Into Practice

I cannot hear. I cannot hear your silence anymore, my Lord. I am deaf.

How can this be? Is it that concern for the world has overcome my soul, choking it of its life's breath? Is it that sin has replaced the purity needed to be in your presence? I do not know. But I know it is as if I am in a desert, removed from your sight. And so my spirit is not nurtured by your light. And so I am deaf. And so I am blind. And so I am dying; most certainly, I am dying… O let me not be dead!

How shall I return to you, O Lord? What shall I do? To find your hand upon my soul once more – let me come back to you.

There must be a way. I know it is not far from me. I know you are always near, always at the door… always in my heart and upon my tongue – if I could but speak your Word, if I could but remember your NAME.

Let your silence overwhelm me, Lord, that I shall never leave, never be apart from thee, never find myself without breath, dying from a lack of your love. O let me hear! Let me listen to your voice.

Still my tongue, O Lord. Still my tongue.

Share with me your love!

On Entering In...

**"My soul waits for the Lord
more than sentinels wait for the dawn."**
Ps.130:6

This quote is from the psalm of the day's Mass (Thurs. of the 28th Week in Ord. Time, Year I). Also in today's readings, Paul tells us, "We hold that a man is justified by faith apart from works of the law" (Rm.3:28). And in our Gospel Jesus chastises a lawyer, "You have taken away the key of knowledge. You yourselves did not enter and you stopped those trying to enter!" (Lk.11:52). But it is the second reading in the Office of the day which most pertains to the point at hand.

I woke in the night late (again) to come into the presence of the Lord and speak His silent NAME. I have been concerned in recent days, as I prepare a version of my horarium for copyrighting/publishing, with finding its proper form. I have struggled in particular for a very long time with waking at 2 a.m. for Vigil prayer. I have been quite unable to be punctual, and the reason has escaped me. But as I began prayer this early morning, the Lord gave me light to realize the source of my difficulty.

Even when I first began seriously to develop this horarium – I believe it was at the time of making the Vigil hour a permanent component – the Lord was reluctant to give approval. Though the Blessed Mother interceded for me, knowing my need for such discipline, He wanted not for me to make an idol of these hours. And our Mother herself gave word that without love, discipline is useless. The Lord only relented with my assurance that I should not be concerned if the hours were taken from me.

And so, as I again struggled to enter into the Lord's silence this night, it came to me clearly that I should treasure this time (this twenty minutes set aside to sit with no other duty but to be with God) more than any other time... and that this should be more than needed to drive me from bed happily. But I realized, too, that I did *not* treasure this time as I should, as would be wise.

Every spare moment, in fact, every lull in activity, should be cause for a certain rejoicing, for it is in this waiting time that we may draw closest to the Lord. But I do not do this – so preoccupied with the practice of prayer and work have I become. Even in church just yesterday I felt without purpose as for ten minutes before Mass I had nothing to do, having already completed all my prayer and reading and writing...

III. Into Practice

We must love the Lord. This is what matters most. If we love the Lord, if we truly desire Him, we will long to be in His presence and treasure any opportunity to be alone with Him. If not, all will become a task, and all be done quite in vain. (How often do we look toward the end of prayer even at its beginning?)

If it were my desire to be with God, then I should long for nothing more than to speak His NAME, for this is the greatest practice of the faith we can know here on earth. But this desire is lacking.

Then (in a most singular moment) I came upon St. Augustine in the Office. He spoke exactly to my thoughts and feelings and understanding. He elucidated clearly this love that draws us to God (who draws all to Himself). It is "not by necessity, but by desire" we come to Him. Here is a whole paragraph of the saint's inspired wisdom:

> Show me one who loves; he knows what I mean. Show me one who is full of longing, one who is hungry, one who is a pilgrim and suffering from thirst in the desert of this world, eager for the fountain in the homeland of eternity; show me someone like that, and he knows what I mean. But if I speak to someone without feeling, he does not understand what I am saying.

I am afraid I have been too much like one without feeling, without *affection* – a word (in the Latin) the priest discusses this morning in his homily addressing the need for both faith and works, and particularly that our practice as Catholics must have love of God. The early love has greatly passed from me; I pray it not pass from you.

And I pray that you will pray for me. It is not simply out of humility I say I do not practice well what I preach – it is the truth. But I have hope that the pride and selfishness, the anger and lust and foolishness which keep me from knowing the Lord (and which anyone who knows me well knows I possess), shall pass away... and I come into God's presence.

Do pray for me, for though the Lord bless me with this most profound understanding of His NAME itself, it does not mean I am any closer to realizing its grace than anyone else; I am, I fear, one of those furthest from His face.

God love you!

1.

Sylvia

God says to man:
   You are my tabernacle;
   you are the place on earth I make my home.
Man says to his wife:
   You are my tabernacle;
   you are the place on earth I make my home.

For "God created man
   in His image" (Gn.1:27)
 and "out of 'her man'
   woman has been taken" (Gn.2:23).

© 2005
James H. Kurt

III. Into Practice

Epigraph

**In this wilderness
I make my home
upon this plane.
There is a home in heaven
that waits for me,
that waits for us all.
But here on this plane,
in this wilderness I make my home.**

1. Sylvia

A Dialogue

Jesus, how shall I begin to understand
your call for my life?

Would you understand, James?

Forgive me, Lord, if I do not come to you with an open heart.
Heal my reticence to hear your word.

If you would understand, I would help you to see,
that you might no longer be so confused.

I do not wish to remain confused, Lord.
I want to see. Help me.

It is not easy, James.
You must trust.

Help my unbelief, O Lord!
Calm my fears. Prepare my heart to receive your word.

I love you, James.

I know this is so, Lord.

But do you trust in my love for you?

Forgive my lack of trust, Lord,
my failing to accept your love.

III. Into Practice

If you would know my love
and live in my love,
then open your heart to my word.

Yes, Lord.
Speak, your servant is listening.
Breathe your Spirit upon me.
The will of your Father be done.

Do not be afraid to love, James.
Do not run from my gifts to you.
The Cross will not be missing.
I love you.

I love you, Lord.

1. Sylvia

A Poem

There is a gift here that God gives me,
a consolation amidst the troubles of this place –
a love to see me through.

I would fight against the grace,
so used to the companion of disappointment,
of rejection and the fruit of bitterness…

But, still, the Lord offers His gift,
holding it out to me
despite the hardness of my heart
toward the love He desires
to impart.

Do not ask how I can be so foolish.
Do not question my fearing His blessing.
Rather, look upon your own soul
and ask,
"In what way do I fail to allow
His love to work in my life?"

And let us pray for one another.

III. Into Practice

I

1.

We are all beaten down by the afflictions of this corrupted world. Assailed by the fruit of our own sins or the consequences of others', we cover our heads and cry, praying the adversary will just go away.

Some harden themselves against the affront of the enemy, pretending mastery even as their hearts crumble; others make the Cross into a trophy – a thing to be displayed in a case.

But all are beaten down by the afflictions of this corrupted world, not knowing how to face the growing tide of relentless attack upon the dignity of our person, not accepting that love alone will heal all our ills.

And so, on we go in disguise, medicating our emptiness by whatever means we find at hand, available over the counter or through the airwaves of moral decay and divine dissent – buying whatever elixir the false prophets tender.

But God alone is our hope, of course. Jesus alone holds the answer. And the answer is the love He offers – but who has faith to hear what the Spirit says?

2.

If one is in misery and handed a mirror, the natural reaction will be to turn away – who wants to see himself as he is when he is humiliated? But who can overcome his desperate state without looking in the mirror?

And so the conflict arises, so the confusion is set in place: how can we face our desperation, a condition repulsive and breeding death; yet how can we afford not to come to terms with what has taken hold of our corrupted souls?

The answer is not easy. The solution is not ready, like a pill we might pop or an ideology we might raise blindly to stand upon the pedestal of our idolatrous thinking… God is not a facile thing, moved at our whim or petulant desire.

Truth is deeper, my friend. Deeper than the surface image of a TV screen or pat response to an overwhelming problem. The mirror that reveals what our souls need to see cannot be bought or sold, or made to comply with our own understanding of what should be. It simply is.

But who can accept this? Who would even care to know? Who would overcome the state into which we've fallen, particularly when it means such pain? Is it not better to remain mired in corruption than to seek and receive love? Who can bear life growing within?

III. Into Practice

3.

Let me ask a question as we begin our book – do you really wish to know the truth; do you really want to find His love? If not, then there is no point in reading on. If not, there is no point in continuing to breathe. Life is quite pointless without this desire for truth... life is quite empty without love.

For this alone you were created: for happiness God has destined you. But one is never happy apart from what is genuine – if not right, you will fall quickly into what is wrong.

But so many souls have no concern for what is right, what God decrees. They would sooner make their own reality and anoint its supposed verity. But no amount of supposition or condescension, no measure of contrivance will make what is not in God's will right in His eyes... and so these false idols will not stand in His light; and so to dust they will soon crumble.

There is but one King, there is but one Lord. Jesus is the way and the truth and the life. None other. Only He leads souls to the Father, to Him who has made us out of the clay of the earth. And none will be happy till he looks upon His face, for none will know himself otherwise; and so, vainly will man seek, in blindness toil all his days, until he looks upon the loveliness of his Lord and God. (Come to this truth, my friend.)

4.

Happiness does await all souls. So the Lord has decreed. But is happiness your desire as it is His?

Happiness seems so far off in this world. It is a world where souls often laugh though more prone to cry. Their joy is not genuine because it is not rooted in God. It is empty, anxious; not wholehearted.

We would do better to cry; it would be more natural, more in keeping with our state... truer. But instead a vain merriment emerges which drowns the soul in the pleasures of this life.

Yet happiness does await. The Lord is not far off at any time. Even in our vanity He calls us to Him. In our tears He seeks to bring His comfort and peace. Our being with Him is always His desire.

Will we turn to what He wills? Will His joy become our own? Will we order our lives according to His word, His word of love and truth, or strike out on our own?

What words do you offer Him this day? Is there a prayer in your heart? Will you seek what He seeks and come to Him on your knees, even as a little child... or remain in your blindness?

The happiness of the Lord is only known in the subjection of our wills to His own. Let us not be apart from His plan for our lives – let our hearts this day be filled with His love.

III. Into Practice

5.

What is this wound that keeps us from looking upon the light that is the face of God? What is the heartbreak that keeps our heads turned down to the ground, hiding our souls in this dark prison? What is the anguish we cannot express that makes love seem a vain endeavor? How will we abandon what we hold to so desperately?

The wound is deep. The human race is far from God. Deeper each day man digs his grave, sure that there is no purpose to life. He bleeds within, a scar forms, and the wound hardens, as if of stone. How can what is done to him and what he has done ever be forgot? How can the stench of death leave his nostrils?

A hopelessness settles in. A certain ennui. What meaning is there to anything? What have we but the dark night?

But in the dark night new life must be sought. Upon this empty ground water must fall; a seed must be planted, if only very small. A prayer must be breathed out, asking for healing of this wound upon our soul. But a word turned toward our Maker is enough to begin His flight to our side. Even in the deepest pit His light does shine, if we would but care to crack an eye, offer a slit in our callused mind.

He calls you, too, my brother, to His love. He will not easily leave you behind. His reach is never-ending and all-encompassing… and the love in your heart He desires.

1. Sylvia

6.

"Put faith in God's love," the priest says after I confess my sins. I seek a word from the Lord, and He provides. Here is the foundation of our Christian lives.

This is balm for my soul, and the soul of every man. None can live without the love of God – our next breath would be impossible without His care. Insofar as we fail to trust in Him, this far are we apart from Him… and so, living in fear.

And fear is that which chokes the soul, that which wounds the heart. To each of us He says, "Do not be afraid," for each of us He would hold in His arms. We must trust ourselves to His love.

I do this here in my writing: I write without revision, trusting that each word is from His mouth. I do not consider beforehand what to say, but get a word and go on His prompting. The Spirit indeed takes care.

But in my life continually I question; His love is not so present in the course of my day – what I do hour to hour I do not readily trust into His hands.

And so comes confusion. And so comes pride. And so judgment is upon my soul, for I do not put faith in the love of God. And apart from Him, where are we, my friend?

We cannot afford to leave His side, for thus we die. (Thus we die.) Thus our next breath becomes a torture and a trial: without His love indeed we die. Put faith in His love and find your life!

III. Into Practice

7.

God is love. So the great Evangelist, he who has seen and has touched love walking amongst us, tells us. And he calls us to love.

If we are called to love, then we are called to God, and if to God then to love – there is no distinction to be made. Love is of God and we are of God only insofar as we are of love. But how do we find love? Here is the question that troubles the darkened mind of modern man, who has turned so far from the light that is God's love to the works of his own hands.

If we would rediscover the pure, simple, ever present love of God, we must necessarily turn in measure from the love we pretend to create, from the false light we make by our own hands, by the poisoned mind of man. God's ways are far above our ways, as are His thoughts – as is His love – and how can we come to know that which transcends all if eternally preoccupied by what we see, by what lies at our feet (or hovers above our heads)?

God is love and we of ourselves are far from that love. To find what we have lost – our very souls, our very lives – we must enter the wilderness, we must be purged of what has been raised around us to stand in the place of that love. Then, cleansed of darkness, cleansed of the colors that appeal to the eye, a pure light we shall find, burning simply in our heart and in our homes.

II

1.

The Lord calls me now, later in life, to marriage, in order to teach me to love. I had finally found my place as a hermit (albeit in the city) after a long struggle, but at least in measure He calls me from this wilderness, from this solitude, to a shared solitude in another wilderness – a wilderness with my loved one, whose name is Sylvia.

Alone I have been most of my life, though not without mistakes in search for marriage. Ever had I been rejected in past proposals; but now my proposal is unconditionally accepted, welcomed and cherished. There has been some question in my own heart, having, as I said, become accustomed to a call to eremitic life – can a hermit marry? – but gradually my resistance to such a change subsides, and I see that this is in the will of God.

So often I have thought I was in love; so often I have thought myself called to be alone. Now in some remarkable way I find myself called to both. I have asked Sylvia to join me in my hermitage, though perhaps I do not understand what I propose, and she has agreed. What shall become of our life together I cannot say, I do not know; but I pray it is only in the hand of God.

2.

The hermitage *is* a place of solitude, a place of prayer – a place where one is alone, alone with the Lord. But as I have said in other writings, the hermitage is a place primarily within; if one does not find this place of silence within oneself, it will not matter where one dwells or how far behind one leaves the world. And I can't help but remember that in marriage two become one. So I am left with the question: Can this *one* be a hermit, a single pray-er before the Lord? Would it be possible to so unite two souls that their prayer rises up as one voice to God's throne?

Perhaps this is a foolish thought, I do not know. Perhaps it is my desiring to hold on to that which is in measure being taken from me – perhaps it again shows my lack of resolve toward marriage. Or perhaps this prayer union will be as a child.

My wife will be beyond the age of bearing children. There will be no fruit of this kind in our marriage. (Another reason I had doubted a call to marriage – would it not be more grace-filled for Sylvia to retain her virginity, and would we not serve the Lord better as separate souls, as has been indicated by the great Apostle Paul?) But if indeed called by God to wed, there must be some fruit to this state… Spiritual works are indeed as children that shall care for us in our old age, in the time of the coming of the Lord; writing books or performing works of mercy certainly may aid in the formation of growing offspring of the Father… but could it be that the crown of such fruit might be a kind of perfection of the unitive purpose of marriage in the making of one hermit offered to God?

3.

"Fear is not of God." This is the word to me in my latest Confession. If the spirit produces fear, if it makes us anxious, the spirit is from other than God. And so, under its influence, I am of other than God.

Why so afraid? Why so anxious? Why so doubtful? Yes, I want to be sure. Yes, there are signs that seem to be warnings to my soul, seem to be answers to my prayers. But still, there is no need of fear, nor of anxiety.

I must surrender all into the Lord's hands. This is the only answer; there is no other way. I can attempt to search out His ways, His words – and indeed our soul must always be set upon these – but it is He who must move me, Him whom I must trust.

And so, into His hands I pray I commend my spirit, commend my life, that He might take all evil from me and enable me to live in the peace of His presence all the days of my life and at every moment of my day. No other way will I find His way than by giving all over to Him.

Then fear will flee. Then this disturbance of mind and heart and soul will be no more. For in this trust is health – in this trust is the way we must walk.

III. Into Practice

4.

Even this day (the one following the previous entry's), John tells us in the readings that "love is not yet perfect in one who is afraid" (1Jn.4:18). And God's judgment cannot be taken from one who still fears.

We must love one another to be of God. It is for this, Jesus has come: to take away all punishment for sin that we might know the love of God and share in that love. As long as we remain in fear, we remain in doubt – Jesus we do not truly believe, and so we remain in sin. And so, how can His Spirit be upon us? And so, how can we be saved?

I am trying to put faith in the Lord, to put all things in His hands – to trust in His love for me and so love others, particularly Sylvia. The devil whispers fear into my heart; whether he invents lies entirely or uses a measure of truth in the process, it is deception that is at his heart, and as long as I listen to him I remain in fear. And God's love is far from me.

But as I open myself to the Lord's love, without fear, without a care for being hurt but only in love itself, then the fear does begin to flee… and the devil has no hold over me.

I shall see her tomorrow for the first time in two and a half weeks. May the Lord be with me and may I trust in His love.

5.

There have been other women. Those whom I should never have approached, those who should never have approached me. Those who should have been as my sister. And so the confusion. And so the fear.

How could I who have been so corrupt accept a gift so pure, and so purely given. Yes, the Lord has come to forgive, to give His love freely to those who do not deserve it, who could never merit it... but still – I have been so corrupt. And how can one fully escape one's past?

Yet if we do not have faith that this is possible, no, that this is *necessary* – and not just for those like myself who have been so obviously the prodigal son of a gracious Father, but for *every* soul – then what shall become of us (for none could get to heaven on his own merit)?

I must believe. I must believe, or I am lost. I must accept God's love, God's forgiveness and mercy... His free gift.

All is but a gift. Life is a gift. Your next breath is a gift. You do not merit any of it, except that God wills it. Take what He gives you, and you will find peace.

III. Into Practice

6.

When have I ever been a man? Ignorant of my responsibilities toward my younger sister, failing as a friend to women who needed my care, and now, at least to some extent, sinful in my conduct as a fiancé.

A man is head of a woman. Though our society would tell us otherwise, even a modicum of common sense, but a glimpse of natural law, tells us it cannot be denied without serious repercussion, without falling further into a culture of death.

It is the man's responsibility to lead the woman; it is upon his shoulders this call from God rests. Thus it is Adam's sin we bemoan and not Eve's. For if he had been an upright man, he would have corrected his wife, interceded for her with the Lord, and kept the blessedness of our race alive.

But he fell, as now so many of us do – and blithely, too. How unlike Christ, who suffered and died for His faithless bride, we are. Though His beloved ever be weak, though we ever stand in need of salvation, the Son of Man does not abandon us... and does not participate in our sin.

I have failed miserably; this I can say without hesitation. Though my pride would hide it from my eyes, in prayer the Lord graces me with truth. Corrupt myself, I have corrupted others, and the chief among these have been women.

7.

Will I be able to stand up straight? This is the question. Will I leave such irresponsibility as has pervaded my relationships with women and be a man, leading souls and the soul of my bride only to righteousness, only to truth? Or will I continue to fall to the devil's lies?

How can a blind man see? How can someone as weak as I be made strong and lead others aright? How can a man who is but a boy, but a child, work in the fields under the hot sun with Jesus Christ?

With Jesus Christ. Certainly this is the answer. There is no other way. Alone I would only continue to stumble, continue to fall... but by His grace and through faith in Him I can be made whole.

Yes, this is our call: to walk with the Lord. Let all men take up their cross, this blessed weight granted to us by God. Or we will certainly fall. And fall not just for ourselves.

How many children are without fathers, how many mothers without husbands? And so our schools are turned upside down, our culture, our life, our days, inverted... and we follow along a path to destruction. Each of us must stand up straight and do the will of the Lord.

III. Into Practice

III

1.

Home. Our home is in heaven. Only there will we take our eternal rest, will we know the everlasting warmth of our Lord and God. Only there do we eat and find ourselves fully satisfied.

But as we have the table of the Lord here on this earth in the Sacrament of the altar, as even here we partake of the Bread of the angels and so gain a foretaste of heaven… so there is a home, a heart, even in this world, where we may take refuge and find ourselves secure in the love of God.

This is primarily the Church, of course; nothing surpasses the open arms of our Mother. But to each of us God grants a place to live, a place where we find ourselves close to Him.

A monk has his cell, a priest his parish, the nun her cloister walls… and to the married man who is blessed, who walks God's way, is granted a good woman in whose arms he might find the Lord's peace.

Work may be a refuge for all souls, as can be family and friends, but in a special way God provides a man with his wife – and to her he clings, if he has sense in his head.

A woman offers rootedness to a man. She it is who holds protection and care, whose eyes and heart are ever looking out to nourish and make a home for the soul entrusted to her. And the man must accept this grace of God.

1. Sylvia

2.

Purity. Oh how the quest for chastity must be our essential call! For only the pure of heart see God, and so, who will come to his eternal home in heaven if not pure?

I love you, Lord, and I wish to love you with a love that is so pure, that is meet to the purity you own. I would be chaste, but here on earth how can one be as thou art, O Lord? Give me the means, dear God, to be as I was at the time of my conversion – to be innocent as a child once more. Increase this grace beyond what I can conceive.

Can you do this in marriage, O Lord? Can you do this in me though I do not abstain from sexual contact with another soul? May marriage be such a blessed state that it could surpass anything I've known of purity alone?

It does not seem possible to my limited mind, O Lord, and perhaps I ask too much. I know there is no love greater than a virgin's dedication to you, Lord, but is it not so that all are most blessed when they fulfill their call? And do you not bless marriage – is it not a sacrament of your Church?

It is, of course, and can and must be pure. Only give me the grace and strength, Lord, to be perfect in chastity and know the great blessings that flow from this way of love in you.

III. Into Practice

3.

The call to holiness is a call to all souls, regardless of station in life. It does not matter whether priest or nun or single or married; in every state we are called to be holy. And if not holy, then we are not of God, whatever our call may be.

"This night your soul is required of you" (Lk.12:20), my brother, my sister. This above all we should keep in mind. The Lord is present now and always, and always calling us to be holy as He, ever commanding us to do His will – what matters is how we respond, now, today, this moment.

It is not easy for the mind and heart and soul of man to grasp the presence of the eternal God and serve Him as He calls. In a sense, it is impossible, at least here on this earth with all our frailties and limitations. But it is something to which we must continually strive, or else we die.

We cannot set aside God's call for a day or an hour; our vocation as Christians demands constant obedience to the Lord. He is our life, our very breath: removed from Him, we cease to exist.

And so, no vow or ordination, no talent or fruit, is sufficient to secure our place in the hand of God. Heaven ever requires our vigilance, calls us to holiness, and keeps us safe only insofar as we comply.

This day pursue a holiness of life and accomplish what the Lord asks of you.

4.

We are temples of the Holy Spirit, are we not? And in a special way a man's wife is a temple – a temple where God dwells. For God dwells in all His creatures, and those purified in Baptism and in communion with His Church are blessed by the Spirit and home to the Lord in a particular fashion… and the virgin bride of a man in a particular fashion is as Christ's holy Bride, the Church.

So to what degree should a man respect his wife! With what measure of reverence should he not approach the bridal chamber. His wife is a temple, he himself is a temple, and God expects due reverence and respect for and from His creatures – and so much more in their union in marriage.

The consummation of the sacred vows of holy Matrimony must be treated with the same awe with which they are to be taken. Given into the hands of God, husband and wife are now one in the Lord, and nothing should diminish their sanctity.

Marriage is a state of worship of the one holy and true God, a vocation to be held up as a sacred sign of His love in the world. Let the man come to his wife as he would a temple, and the Lord will be honored as He should.

III. Into Practice

5.

It is the feast of the Presentation of the Lord in the temple at Jerusalem, the day the light was brought to the Church of God; into these walls built by hands but blessed by the Almighty comes the Son of Man, comes our salvation.

And we, too, must be given to the Father as was His Son. We too are to offer ourselves to God through the hands of Mary. I think of the religious, of course, who dedicate themselves so completely to the service of the Lord and His Church; but, again, it is all souls that are His, and to Him they must be given.

Light to the world must every Christian soul be, without exception. Our candles must burn brightly before God and before our fellow man. Who is exempt from such a duty; where is it the Lord's light does not reach?

I wonder mostly this day just how a married man can give himself as completely as a religious. Do I but daydream, or can he fall prostrate as those who wear the habit? Will his offering be as acceptable, his and his wife's?

O Lord, purge my soul from all evil. Take all darkness from me by your holy light. That I might be pure. That I might know you and love you and serve you as every child ought.

6.

To maintain one's purity is not an easy thing. It is a cross. And if one does not accept the cross then one will inevitably lose himself in the struggle – for the devil will have the advantage.

We do not wish to struggle. We do not think we should need to fight. All should be easy – let God take care, we say. But it is *our* life, our will He gives us... a share in His own freedom. And this freedom requires our participation, requires the proof of our desire to be with Him.

But we are weak. Yes, we are weak, it is true; but God makes us strong – this we should not forget. When we call upon Him, He is with us... and the devil is no match for His power. By the Lord we overcome the flesh and the world.

But we must have faith. We must have faith and the desire to do what is right, what is according to His will... what is holy and pure. If our head is turned by the temptations of this world and our flesh follows easily on this wayward path, who will save us? If it is our desire to sin and so to die, what can the Lord do? He will not tie our hands.

Let our hearts be set on His call and prepared well for the cross. Let us even take joy in the trials our living in Christ brings.

7.

It is Ash Wednesday. A blessed day, a beginning of purgatorial penance and preparation for the kingdom. A time so necessary to the human soul.

There is something in us that must die. Who is without sin? And so to be reminded of this, how anointed we are; for if not, would we not forget, would we not grow accustomed to our sin?

And so, how would we conquer the lust that destroys our purity, our singleness of heart and mind? How would we remove the anger from our tongues and the pride that inflates our souls? Would not these devils take control?

No way would we find to peace if not repentant. This is the fundamental call of the Lord – repent and believe for the kingdom is at hand. And if we would enter there, we must be cleansed of the things of this earth which keep us rooted to the flesh and apart from God's Spirit.

There is a peace that awaits us. Let us be redeemed by Jesus' blood, pouring through us to take away all sin.

IV.

1.

I am to be married in three months; how necessary this Lent is to my preparation. For I am still not ready. I am still not pure in thought, word, and deed. And to enter in as I am would not be fruitful.

But the Lord gives me the grace of these forty days to repent specifically in preparation for my marriage vows. I need to find greater discipline, first of all, about my hours, about my prayer and work, for sloth regarding this leads to other sins, and adherence to this cross sets my days right.

I must guard my tongue as well, for speaking too much indeed sets the soul on fire, burning with an unholy flame. I must hold my tongue against judgment, against foolish speech, against a pride that kills the soul. Silence is so necessary to the sanctification of one's life, and I have not been set in it – I too often forget the NAME of God.

And my eyes and my hands must yet be controlled; they must not be given reign to do as they please, or how shall I maintain purity? How shall that chastity so germane to a holy marriage be mine if lust has any place in me? No illicit act can be done if one is to find oneself wed to the only Son.

III. Into Practice

2.

I am not a man. How can I be if I repeatedly fall into sin? Three days into Lent and my resolve is shaken. Yes, I repent in tears. Yes, I am sincere. But still I fall.

I am not a man. How can I be, weak as I am? If one leads a woman into sin, is that one a man? That is a soul fit for the dung heap.

A man is called to be dignified, to be virtuous, to be strong – to lead souls that are with him down right paths where refreshment waits. A man must be holy, or he is no man at all. He might as well be a dog.

I wish I were a man. May the Blessed Mother pray that I shall be so. May healing flow forth to redeem me of my sin, that I might stand with Jesus Christ, the only Man worth emulating.

No man is worthy of the name who cannot control his hands and tongue – let him rather be cast into prison where there is hope he may be purged. Heaven has no place for the selfish heart.

1. Sylvia

3.

Valentine's Day is passed, and a resolution seems to have come between Sylvia and me, to better avoid the near occasion of sin. It is I, of course, who need most to abide by its terms, but without terms and without clear consent from both of us, I would certainly soon be lost; for any excuse I can make I will allow entrance and acceptance.

There are so many excuses, are there not? Look at the world today – where is a soul concerned for maintaining chastity even among strangers, how much less between those engaged to be wed? And so, how easy it is to fall into the ways of the culture, especially when one has in the past been such a part of that culture, as is so for myself.

But the struggle must be commenced, or we are already lost, already numb to sin and its deadly consequences. If we give in, there is little hope for grace and truth to fill our lives. And so, weak as I am, I pray a certain understanding between us will help Sylvia and me avoid falling into sin.

To give ourselves to the Lord is our desire. I pray we will not fall short of living truly in Christ. I pray we shall indeed be temples of the Holy Spirit and not give God lip service alone.

III. Into Practice

4.

How I need to turn from my sin; how difficult it is. But thank the Lord that He gives us all opportunity to do so and enter into His blessings and glory.

The Lord promises in the Scriptures this day that whoever turns from sin will be acceptable to Him, and He will remember that man's sin no more. How I need to trust in this word! For my past seems still with me and I find it difficult to forget what I have done.

So many hearts I have hurt, for so foolish have I been, so blind to the truth and walking in ways against God's will. Yet all the while I made excuse. All the while I continued forward on wrong roads that led only to further sin, refusing to listen to what was told me or consider how far afield I had gone.

We cannot presume, brothers and sisters. We cannot presume against the teachings of the Church and God Himself that what *we* think is right if it seems good to us, or that what we don't understand we can leave aside. We must be obedient to our guide, or indeed end lost in this world.

There are many temptations in this culture of death. Take refuge we must in the Lord's Cross.

5.

Hermit in the city. This is what I am, what I would term myself. And Sylvia will join me in my hermitage, and we will be nothing together.

Nothing. Can there be a greater call than to be nothing before the Lord? Not long after we met, Sylvia and I stated our nothingness, and even had a playful argument about who was more nothing. To be nothing in this world is to be everything for God.

In the quiet, in the stillness, we must find Him – for it is only in silence He speaks. And when we open our mouths, He is quick to leave.

To be holy is to be set apart, apart, of course, from the corruption of this world, even if living in its midst. And this is our call. This is God's call to every soul: to be with Him, to be with Him despite and through the circumstances. In all things we must give ourselves to the Lord.

His peace descends upon my soul now, as I give it and everything to Him. As reparation I make for my sins, He comes to make His home with me. May His home be made complete.

III. Into Practice

6.

What if the Lord placed the most beautiful creature on earth in your arms – what would you do? Would you take her and corrupt her with the lust in your heart? Would you hand her back to the Lord, where she belongs, unable to accept such a gift? Or would you accept the gift with grace and thanksgiving?

She belongs with you, does she not, Lord? I am but a sinful man. Would it not be better I remain celibate, and she a virgin for you? Could we not both serve you better in this way? O Lord, how wonderful your purity is! Let us not despoil it.

Help me, Lord, for I do not understand – yet do I struggle to know your call. Perhaps a celibate marriage? The idea brings a certain peace. But would she accept, and is this your will?

I do not know, Lord. I do not know. It seems these words are ingrained upon my lips. I do not know, but let me trust in you. Please, let your will be done.

I would remain alone. Yes, I would prefer this cross, I think. But my hands are open to receive what you offer. Only do let your nails pass through them, that I and all in my care may come to your kingdom.

7.

I suppose the answer is obvious to everyone. It even begins to become clear to me: I must accept the gracious gift of the Lord with thanksgiving. He leaves me no choice, really. This happiness is His will. (And I believe it is the will of Sylvia as well.)

The Lord provides. Though we turn from His provision because of selfishness or foolishness, His hand does continue to reach out to us – He will not leave us alone. And we would do well to seek and trust in His grace.

It is not easy for any of us, I know, to accept His gracious will, to receive His love. It seems we are undeserving, it seems an illusion… so many cannot simply trust. And so they turn to empty paths, vain ways of making their lives in this world, when all that is needed is a small measure of faith. Then light would come to all of us, however distant from His love we may feel.

To be obedient to Him is to be free. If we do not serve Him, whom do we serve but the world and the flesh? – and ultimately become the slave of the devil. Can't you see this, my brother, my sister? Only in Him are we ourselves; only in Him are we free… for only He releases us from fear.

You are love, O Lord, and all who seek love and peace come to you; and none of these do you leave alone. I thank you, Lord, for your grace, for your care… for the life you give to me and all of your children. Make us one in you, dear God.

III. Into Practice

An Epilogue

Here, I see,
the cross will not be lacking.
And so I embrace this call
from the Lord.

2.

A Third Pilgrimage

May 2005

© 2005
James H. Kurt

III. Into Practice

FEVER

(5/20/2005, 3:33 a.m.)

This first night in Medjugorje I've woken with a fever – or so Sylvia tells me after feeling my head and neck. As I sit in the bathroom with my feet on a wet towel – having come here to pray – I only know I have had a most intense dream… one which encourages me not to be afraid as I glide above the crocodiles through the island brush.

There was a prayer I spoke to the sky, and its miraculous clearing. There was my helping a woman remove a long-standing stain from a floor… and this night I write for the first time in a long while. Then the gliding to and through the island, with each further passage my stating the obstacles and then saying, "But I am not afraid."

The devil would have us think the worst of souls, to blame them for the evil that befalls us through his workings. But I do not speak ill of anyone, whether a cousin, brother, wife, mother, or friend, nor the people of Medjugorje or any soul near or far – and I have a request: that should I die here, I be buried here, though it must be in sacred ground. And to my wife and brother I leave all things, including this.

DAY 2

Be not afraid. Each day of the year, trust in Him.

A fearful dream, pursued by enemies who would cut me to pieces, and seem to. But there is a refuge in this world, a friend.

And the two shall become one, by the grace of God. May it be so with my wife and me. May the Lord bless us even here with His presence in our lives.

Mama Mary, please pray for us and bless our pilgrimage and marriage. Let it be sanctified by the Cross of your Son and find fulfillment through you.

III. Into Practice

PART HONEYMOON

Saturday

Father Svetozar handed me a cherry as we walked along after his talk this day: "I should give you one of these."

This pilgrimage is also a honeymoon, a time to get to know and love the treasure of a wife the Lord gave me but one week ago. And tonight we have ice cream. And this day we climb Mount Krizevic, me with bare feet and wobbly legs. And today, too, we make love.

The cross of marriage can be sweet, but it must always be a cross, it must always be of Christ. And the Blessed Mother must always be present, as she is here in this sacred land – where the Rosary and the Mass are heard around the village every evening, on the radio and even through loudspeakers; here where thousands gather outdoors for adoration of the Blessed Sacrament… this must be as our marriage, holy and true and devout.

May the Lord purify me now to live a marriage blessed by His grace, even as tears course down my face as I kneel before Him, as the priest raises His Presence in the monstrance to bless us.

2. A Third Pilgrimage

VOCATION

How is the Lord calling me? Really, there are so many questions that remain; so much confusion still reigns. About my marriage, about my prayer, about my writing… about my life in and for the Lord. Yet do I hope and pray for clarity, for answers.

I have felt more comfortable, more at ease, more at home on this pilgrimage with my wife. But there are things I do still need to know. Will the Lord God give me His light through the intercession of His Blessed Mother?

It is Trinity Sunday – God's Day. His NAME is spoken in our first reading and His salvation recounted in our Gospel. There is a special blessing of peace just spending three hours with Him and His people in prayer in church… He comes close. But still.

What is my vocation, Lord? How do you call me? Open my mind and my heart, soul and body, to you. Move upon me, Holy Spirit, I pray.

III. Into Practice

HER SON

I have been seeking someone to talk to, to discuss problems in my soul… perhaps a Confession with Father Svetozar… but have not been successful all day. Yet my Mother has promised that I shall find someone.

At the Blue Cross on Podbrdo Hill this night with my wife and others, I pray in the Spirit to the Lord, speaking His silent NAME, and the Blessed Mother comes to me. She reminds me that I am the Lord's tabernacle, that I may always speak with Him, be with Him… and promises a special blessing.

I doubt this word as the fruit of pride, but try to open myself as a child to what may come. I sense her presence but find nothing special, though all is well. At one point I close my eyes and distinctly feel (and see) the wounds of Christ in my hands…. Here is the promised gift – knowledge of the Cross, of Jesus' love. And I realize Mary always leads us to her Son, and He is known in His sacrifice for us.

2. A Third Pilgrimage

MOON AND SUN ON KRIZEVIC

Early in the morning (3:15) we set out for Krizevic, a full moon over its peak. As we near the mountain, the moon becomes hidden, and is not visible again till we reach the top.

We reach the top still in the dark, but a glow upon the horizon. The wind blows strongly and Syl is cold, but we remain an hour until the sun becomes visible, seeking the Mother's blessing.

Coming down the mountain, the sun illumines all, and gives warmth. (Syl has to take her jacket off.) Everything is beautiful in this land.

III. Into Practice

GOD'S LOVE

It is the night before our departure and we are waiting in church for the adoration hour (and all-night vigil) to begin. A singular experience earlier this evening:

I got in line for Confession – a Confession I had waited several days to make – well before the Rosary was to begin, to be sure I would be in church for the moment of silence at its high point.

I moved a few times to shorter lines, but ended always waiting longer… One priest was with the same penitent about 45 minutes – and I was the next (and only) person in line most of that time.

Finally, I moved back to a previous confessor. I wondered why it had been so difficult to find a confessor, but realized Our Lady must have some purpose… and certainly I placed the Confession into her hands.

As it turned out, I was in the midst of my Confession, just outside the walls of the church, during the moment of silence. And here again was a personal blessing for me. The priest spoke to just what the Lord's word for me has been: that He wants to show me His love (in my relationship with Sylvia) and that I should trust in Him and not look back.

(I would encourage every soul to find the grace the Lord offers every pilgrim.)

CORPUS CHRISTI

The Croats celebrate Corpus Christi on the 26th of May, this Thursday of our departure, rather than on a Sunday. And so we are seen off by this great Solemnity of the Church.

We are all one in Christ and in the Eucharist, all of His Body and Blood. We *are* all one Body, and this is very evident here in Medjugorje, where people of all nations, rich and poor, young and old alike, come together to celebrate their faith in the Lord.

"The holiest place on earth," a priest says, and it is true. Here I would like to remain. For here the Body is not broken – it is whole.

And though I have far to go to realize my oneness with all my brothers and sisters, to take them into myself without prejudice, without judgment – with love – yet I pray I shall… and soon.

Make us one in you, O Lord. All souls are gathered together in your flesh and in your blood.

III. Into Practice

RETURN

We return with throats sore, bodies weak. I seem to be feverish once again [and would, in fact, be sick a month or so].

At Mass in a little chapel this early evening, I sense the same Presence as that which permeates Medjugorje. Every church is the holiest place on earth, for in every church Jesus is present… and He alone is holy.

Bless us, O Lord, all days.

3.
A Married Hermit
a. Love and Discipline

I have, after praying in tears, been granted understanding of the purpose of my marriage – why the Lord has given Sylvia to me: that I not be empty in my discipline, in my practice of prayer; for then all would be worthless… then I would be dead.

It must be obvious (in the horarium especially) that I have a distinct proclivity to define all moments of my day. This is not a bad thing necessarily, and is to be expected of one who strives to be a monk/hermit. But even if the horarium were perfected, it would be quite pointless without love.

Sylvia is quite the opposite of me. She has not regular hours even for work and sleep – working as she does three twelve-hour nights a week (as a nurse), and so sleeping sometimes during the day, sometimes at night, often an hour or two or three here or there… This is but one concrete example of a difference that is much more germane to our natures: she much better at improvising, at adjusting as she goes – and so, I would say, at love; me much more rigorous and defined, more attuned to discipline.

There are those who might favor either side in the quest for a religious life, a way of following Christ, but really, without both, neither is of worth.

And so, the Lord has sent me Sylvia to save me from lifeless works of the law. I must learn to adapt, to adjust (literally, to make true) – this is what love calls us to do as we relate one to another… to move as the waves with the changing tide all the while seeking the way the Lord marks out for us. And ironically marriage takes me not from my hours but closer to their fulfillment.

Peace of Christ.

III. Into Practice

b. Hermit in the Center

The call for me as a hermit in the city seems to be as a soul in the center of the states of life. The hermit is indeed at the center of the Church, the hub of the wheel – the very heart wherein the Spirit breathes… but what I mean here is regarding specifically, as I say, the states of life to which men and women may be variously called.

I am a hermit, yes, but not in the traditional sense of one who goes literally into the desert or wilderness, isolated from the world. This is the hermit in the strictest sense. I think it was in communication with a desert father one day that I best explicated the call I find upon my soul. It was before my marriage and I was trying to explain how a hermit might be married, as well as live in the city. I mentioned the Lord's word to me, "You are my tabernacle," and he was intrigued by this… but how to get across the singularity of this hermit's state?

I see myself spanning all the states, holding out my arms to embrace and live them all in measure enough indeed to get my arms around them more easily. I am married, so this state is clear. Yet I have no children and, barring a miracle, shall have none of my own. I had been single for forty-five years, and lived most of that time much as a religious; here in this book I make my case for recognition of the spiritual life I've found. And as for the priestly vocation – the Church is the center of my life, holy Mass is all to me (to the point of adopting the liturgical colors in my dress); and perhaps the most significant book I have published to date is exposition of the readings for Mass. (Also, who knows – only the Lord – I may one day be a deacon and thus gain the grace of ordination.)

The need to span all the states was driven home to me recently when I was contemplating leaving my one-day-a-week, five-hour class at a local college. With my wife's income, we didn't need the money (there had, in fact, begun to be more money around than I could be comfortable with), and so I thought here was an opportunity to enter into this hermit's state in a more complete manner. I was quite conflicted about the decision though.

3. A Married Hermit

But in the end it wasn't the income or the ability to point to some work that I was accomplishing that kept me teaching. I was prepared to give up these considerations, and had rather decided to go through with the idea. The Blessed Mother called me back to work that I might keep my hand in the "real" world, that I might learn to go through it – to transcend it even while working in it – and to be a sign even for those who toil. It became clear now to me that I must indeed stand in the center of all, a bridge among the stations of life and a sign that every soul can and must find the hermitage within.

III. Into Practice

c. The Universal Call to Holiness

**"In whatever situations we happen to be,
we can and we must aspire to the life of perfection."**
St. Francis de Sales, *Introduction to the Devout Life*
(taken from Office of Readings for the saint's day, Jan. 24)

St. Francis de Sales has warned that if devotion "ever works against, or is inimical to, anyone's legitimate station and calling, then it is very definitely false devotion" (ibid), but at the same time he has counseled that all are called to a life of perfection, of holiness. This has, of course, been confirmed by Vatican II, and so we see that there is nothing inordinate in the idea, the proposal, that every soul should speak the NAME of God, should pray.

It is true, again, that the prayer practice one employs should not "work against" one's more general call or occupation/vocation – it should enliven and perfect it – but it is truer that without a life of prayer, one's vocation (including that of priesthood and religious life) will quickly die, will rot away in vanity. Without breath how quickly the body passes away… Let us never forget that though all may be useful, only "one thing is needful."

Who is there that cannot find moments in the day to adore the Lord? How many Rosaries might a truck driver pray? Who cannot remember the NAME of the Lord, His silent presence, even while waiting at a red light? How many hours do we fritter away in front of the T.V.? – and yet we have no time for daily Mass or regular Confession. How many books and magazines and newspapers are consumed? – and yet we cannot partake of the Word of God, the holy food of Scripture, the Bible. It may not be easy to pray (praise God!) but it is never prevented by our state in life… unless we have simply become too busy, too preoccupied by temporal duties.

I think there can be no busier, more occupied, person than a mother, particularly one with many and young children. Yet, though her arms may be full every hour of the day, even she can practice prayer. She may not have much quiet time to herself, but she can call her children together to recite the Rosary; she can read Scripture to them and expound upon it, performing her primary duty of religious educator even as she practices what I have outlined herein. And she can speak the Lord's NAME while nursing in the night.

3. A Married Hermit

I have been blessed with time and quiet, virtually full-time to devote to God and the practice of prayer. Perhaps the Lord would have me serve as a kind of model as to what can be done. But there is none who cannot incorporate, in whatever measure feasible according to his place and situation, the practices outlined herein… and there is certainly and most importantly no one who has not the time to remember God's NAME. For indeed it is the simplest of things taking the shortest amount of time – one could not even say a second. Though what is most simple, most natural, for man – worship of God – has come to seem most difficult and unnatural because of our sinful separation from His mind and heart, it is no less true that the Lord waits at every moment for us to turn to Him. Take up His call and enter His presence – remember His NAME: YHWH.

Amen.

"We must be silent; it is so simple."
Bl. Elizabeth of the Trinity
(from *The Praise of Glory*, Ch. IX, "The Inner Life")

III. Into Practice

A Final Note:

When the Lord blesses us with any practice of the faith, we should be joyful and look for no further reward. This is reward in itself – for it draws us closer to Him and His love. Only the most spoiled child would expect praise for accepting great gifts from his father. Let us pray only that such gifts be increased.

IV

On Finding A House of Prayer

1. Four Hours
2. Striving

IV. On Finding a House of Prayer

**"If the Lord does not build the house,
in vain do its builders labor."**
(Ps.127:1)

"My house shall be called a house of prayer for all peoples."
(Is.56:7)

A house gives order, a house gives space for light to shine…

    Build me a house in which I may dwell, O Lord my God –

        Let this house be a house of prayer.

An Introduction

There may be a soul whom the Lord shall bless with strict adherence to the hours herein – and that soul may even one day be me... but it is not so today and cannot be for most, lest they tend to make what should lead to recollection, what should lead to the Lord's presence and the fulfillment of His will, into something quite the opposite: something that makes the soul quite anxious and apart from Him, as has been the case with me, at least to some extent. For most there will need to be improvisation upon the theme, perhaps the keeping of the hours, though other works done for the Lord may enter in, ones other than outlined here.

But perhaps some soul, some day, by the Lord's blessing...

The preceding seems to bemoan the inability of the soul who would find the Lord God in his life. But let not all be lost to our weakness, for God will strengthen us as need be, according to His will and our desire to align ourselves with it.

So here is my striving in faith to fulfill His call, to find a spiritual life in Him, to live an order He would ordain. And in the striving is a joy; in the struggle is a refuge and a peace – for the Cross is our home in this world, leading always to the glory of the Lord. And so let us remember His NAME... and find a House of Prayer.

IV. On Finding a House of Prayer

    The NAME of the Lord is upon me again;
    without Him I am nothing –
        my heart a tomb,
        empty and dark...
      Until He breathes upon me,
    until He inspires my soul,
        I have no love.

    But when He speaks,
      when in silence He comes to me,
        His truth piercing
        both hands and spirit –
    then I breathe again
    as one with Him...

        and I am alive;
        and I write.

1.

Four Hours

Holy Hours of written introspection on basic themes

(from two-day private retreat
at San Alfonso Retreat House, in rectory chapel)

© 2006
James H. Kurt

IV. On Finding a House of Prayer

1. Prayer
9/18/06, 4-5 p.m.

A

Prayer. What can be said of prayer? It is first, certainly, as God is first, and must be kept first, always. If one ceases praying, one ceases living, for one loses relationship with the Lord, who is life itself. One may continue breathing, I suppose, but it would be most vain, and only seem to be life. In the end its emptiness is revealed. So let us not remove ourselves from prayer, from intimacy with our God, with the Father of all Creation, and all will be well; and we shall not die.

But in this hour I am to consider more specifically the form prayer ought to take in my life, and how I can better pray – perhaps the latter should be the former here, for prayer itself is more important than the form it takes... and I have not been praying well. Too rushed, too mechanical, too empty. Little real communication with the Lord; just keeping hours. Hours must be kept, no doubt, as long as the clock continues ticking, but we must not be slaves to time. And so the order must be found, must be made clear, though the prayer itself indeed takes precedence at all times.

Perhaps if the form were better defined, or kept to – I speak here specifically of the horarium I've developed – then my soul would be better set on oneness with the Lord. Or is it that I am too concerned with keeping time, and so, as one running to catch a bus, find myself quite out of breath, apart from recollection? I have said that all spiritual practices must lead to recollection, yet how little recollected I often am, and so, are not the practices vain? Ah, may the Spirit give me some light to help me understand the direction my prayer should take!

1. Four Hours

B

If I am to consider prayer, then I should consider first the prayer I have declared as first and all prayer – speaking the Father's NAME. It is this NAME upon which the order I've conceived is founded, and so where else to begin but here? Here is the very heart of prayer; here is the Breath of God, spoken for our ears to hear. Here is that which brings us into communion with Him, and so must be present in all prayer... or it is not prayer at all. And so, if I can better remember the NAME of the Father (my principal call), then I would be better set in order. All else of which I am concerned here and in all these hours would thus fall into place.

Consideration of this prayer should begin where it begins for me, in the particular place and time set apart for it: upon waking in the night for Vigil. Twenty minutes has been set aside for this prayer, for this silence in the presence of the Lord. And though certainly it cannot be relegated to a single moment of the day – as I've said, it must be present in *all* prayer, and so ever present as God Himself – yet here is a beginning, a first step toward its omnipresence in our day. But how far from Him I tend to be at this time; how much of this time is wasted.

And before all prayer, formal prayer particularly, I should remember God's NAME, I should speak the silence that brings me into His presence. Yet here I am more forgetful, I'm afraid, rushing into and through my Hours and Rosary without a thought that He is there.

He is here before me now in the Sacrament. The presence of God is housed in the tabernacle of this chapel. And so should He be housed in me. O Lord, how can I learn to remember? Will you not help me to pray?

You must take the first step before such a journey can begin.

(And so, let me remember His NAME.)

C

It seems there is little left to say after such admonition. The answer is obvious: do as you should, perform the first task, and the others will follow suit. Do not look for more before you have completed the basic requirement. One cannot see tomorrow if one is blind to today. And so, indeed, remember His NAME!

Let it be written upon your soul, engraved upon your spirit by the Hand of God. His Breath must be upon your soul, or, indeed, you will be unable to go on. You wish to know of this or that particular thing – and these questions need to be answered, need to be addressed, resolved – but you do not answer the Lord's fundamental call: Remember His NAME, my brother! All answers are found in His presence.

So let me here pause...

D

It only takes a moment to enter into God's presence, His light, to know His Breath in your heart of hearts – and so to find answer to any question, from Him who knows all.

O Lord, your light upon my mind is overwhelming! Stepping into your presence is – I love you, Lord! You are my God; you are my King. You are all and everything. And I am your child. Let me be your child, dear Father.

O Lord, lead me along your way, along right paths with you. Faith let me have that you are with me and will guide me in all things.

Yes, to live in your NAME you do call me. To hold on to this grace is all I must do. O let me declare your holy Presence, and how close we are called to be with you.

I will find an order on the Cross of your Son. Here on earth let me breathe with your Word upon me – and so, obedient let me be.

2. Marriage
9/19/06, 9:30-10:30 a.m.

A

All that matters is remembering God's NAME, refining one's soul, drawing ever closer to Him so He is always with us. And so why marriage? What of marriage? I see that to ask such a question is to ask why the Cross, or, "Why do we need the Son when we have the Father?" We need the Son.

We need the Son first of all because we are not angels flying about Heaven; we are human beings walking the earth. We have flesh, we have blood, and so we need His flesh and blood to sanctify us. And so we need marriage.

What has marriage to do with Christ? you say. Why do I relate the Son to it? It is of the flesh as He is of the flesh, and must become of the Spirit as is He. Our shoulders are made for such a Cross as this; they are grooved to fit its beam. And without the Cross we are quite empty – without suffering we would not know joy.

His body we eat, His blood we drink, and His presence we become. All this through the gift of the Eucharist; all this through His sacrifice on the Cross. Were He not born unto us, had He not given His life, His death, for our sakes, where would we be, brothers and sisters? Answer to this we cannot give, for we would be too lost to find words to say.

And so let us be wed to one another, and so wed to His Church, for then we will be wed unto Him, into whose Body we are wrought. And let the vows between a man and his wife be the perfect model of this union without which we are not of the Lord.

B

But it is consideration of my own state which is to be the purpose of this undertaking, and so, what of my own marriage? It is true that I would run from it, thinking that apart from it would lie perfection in God.

But this is not the will of the Lord, any more than it is His will that I be an angel. He has made me a man, this should be clear; and He has called me to be married, as I now am. And so to run from it is to run from God, and not closer to Him.

It is indeed this day the purpose of marriage becomes clear to me; as I remember the NAME of the Lord, His Breath upon me brings peace... and my heart begins to beat with a love that had been far from me. The fundamental fact is that the Cross is a joy and so something we should embrace with zeal, to find thus our lives in Jesus. Christ has died for us, has He not? And so, if it were our desire to be like Him, we would run to our own death in the Lord. It should be but our joy to join our Savior in His sacrifice. But how far this desire has been from me.

I have suffered in vain. As I have prayed in vain, so I have offered sacrifice in vain, not taking joy in the Cross. And all this because there has been no real love in my heart – His blood courses not through my veins.

And so I am blind and without purpose, so far apart from God's grace. O Lord, let me embrace your Cross!

C

The Cross is love – it is simple as this. We say that our husband or wife is our cross, as if to say he or she brings us but pain and suffering. But we seem to have no sense that the Cross is the source of our salvation, that it is the glory of Christ... that He embraced it quite willingly and obediently, and with love, and so love has been poured out upon the face of the earth. Should we not desire to join Him in such blessed sacrifice?

Certainly marriage is painful – it is never easy to live with another and to have to die to ourselves, to our own wills and ways, in order to join as one with another heart. But if we cannot do this, we shall be truly dead – as indeed I have been.

I accepted marriage upon the Lord's assurance that the Cross would not be missing (fearing as I had that this would be too easy a life). And now that the Cross is upon me, what do I desire but to set it aside, to cast it away? And so the love of the Lord I would leave behind!

O let me not turn from your love, O Lord, your great love which would purify my soul. Your love which makes real the love of the Father let me never turn away from.

Let me rather thank you, dear God, for this gift you have granted me. With my wife let me become one, one in you and in Jesus your Son. Teach me now to love. May the Word be made flesh in us.

IV. On Finding a House of Prayer

3. Work

9/19/06, 2:30-3:30 p.m.

A

And now, work. Our daily bread: that which sustains us – a sharing in the light of the Spirit and the fulfillment of the kingdom in the world. "If anyone will not work, let him not eat" (2Thes.3:10); and so it is that work is our food. Where would we be without the talents the Lord provides? Dead. Buried in the ground. So let us employ ourselves in the call upon our souls.

Whatever we do may be a blessing, may be a grace, may be a sign of God's presence in this place. Whether sweeping floors or singing songs, all may and must be done for the Lord, and He will be recognized in the task we perform. Small or large does not matter, for He is in all things and all places, and we must be there with Him.

In considering work for my own life, I must consider again prayer and, again, the remembrance of God's NAME. This is the most difficult work, to combat our inherent forgetfulness and enter into the Lord's overwhelming presence. So prayer may be said to be my work.

But all of us must accomplish the work of prayer, all must come to know God and remain in His presence – and all of us are called to an occupation in addition to prayer. My own daily bread is closely aligned with prayer and the life of the Lord; it may be seen in this very writing. I am called to write and to write on prayer and the contemplative life, and so prayer and work may sometimes seem indistinguishable. But this reflection on prayer and the life lived in God is not prayer itself in the ordinary sense. I'm not praying now. Though calling on the Lord in every line to guide me (and so, in a general sense, praying), my nose is to the

1. Four Hours

grindstone and I am a tool to serve at His favor, an instrument (I pray) of God's will.

And so let me pray that I shall ever write, and write well in the Name of our Savior.

B

But all is not well in the working world for me, as it has not been in prayer or marriage. I work not well or with consistency, or with confidence in what I am doing.

I must often question what the Lord calls me to, and if I am accomplishing His will. Many books have I written but few published, and little has this work been shared with the world.

By the power of the Spirit, it is for the world our work is done, for our fellow man and his development. We all must contribute to the growth of the kingdom and bear fruit in the manner called by Christ. But I know in my heart this is not the case with me, though anxiously I may perform certain tasks. I fear what is most necessary is being overlooked for what is simply close at hand. And what of the laziness that causes me to be satisfied with minimal labor for the day? This is not as it should be.

I have a book that has begun to sell, that has found favor with those who have taken it in hand, and it may profit them well... But there is a work which for two years has not been published (and another of the past that still seems neglected, unfulfilled). The book in question [this one] is one on the Divine NAME – and so this overriding theme returns again. Though for twenty years I have been given understanding of its significance (and for five worn the NAME around my neck), and though a few persons I have approached with this insight... still I do not think another soul could relate back to me what I have tried to explain. And its light to this extent remains hidden.

IV. On Finding a House of Prayer

Just this morning I tried, very poorly, to instruct my wife on speaking the NAME... without success. However, although I do not think progress was made in her comprehending what I so feebly tried to convey, yet in this attempt itself, in this work, there was a certain grace given to me.

We must but work and we shall be blessed. Though the work is only for a time in a world that is passing, yet to the eternal fruits of heaven it leads our souls, if to the Lord it is given.

O Spirit of the living God, help me to publish the Father's NAME.

4. House
9/20/06, 10:30-11:30 a.m.

The final hour. A single page. On a topic not quite defined. I thought this entry would be about where to live, a question with my wife and I for the past several months; but I think it is more to do with a House of prayer.

What is this House wherein I should dwell? In these writings on an order based on the Divine NAME, I speak of it specifically as a house. Since last I wrote, less than a day, two priests have counseled me on its foundation, one in great depth. I have never been granted so much attention, and so much sincere prayer, regarding the possibility. One priest spent well over an hour with my wife and I, praying over us and with us in most remarkable fashion – the Holy Spirit very much moving – all culminating in particularly intense Confessions for each of us. And the other priest who kindly spoke to us is a founder of perhaps the most significant order in the Church today. What blessings the Lord has showered upon us! And now I am to go home and speak with another wise priest who promises to become a spiritual director.

1. Four Hours

And so the House is to be a house of prayer. And it is certainly a cross, for, as said, what pain and what joy it is to really come into prayer before the Lord. And, of course, any house I have must accommodate my marriage, my wife, as well. So all these four become one in the end – one as the Trinity is one and we are one with them through our Blessed Mother. But there should be a certain practicality here: the spiritual practices are like the wood with which the house is built. It must be a solid structure set on a firm foundation – set, of course, on the NAME of God. Its walls must be sure and its windows open to the light. And certainly it must always accommodate a refreshing breeze... and have water for washing ourselves clean.

Let it be built, O Lord. Let it be built only in your NAME. Where and when and in the way you lead, let it be built. But let us begin this day, yesterday, in applying ourselves to its steady construction. Day in and day out may our heart be set on building a House for you – that we might become as your temple, living forever in your presence.

IV. On Finding a House of Prayer

– A Bridge –
Eve of the Solemnity of Christ the King
(Sat. of the 33rd Week in Ord. Time)

> "I will give no sleep to my eyes,
> to my eyelids I will give no slumber
> till I find a place for the Lord,
> a dwelling for the Strong One of Jacob."
> Ps. 132:4-5

How I wish I could say these words of myself.
David speaks them of building the temple of the Lord;
every Christian should desire so untiringly
to make of himself a temple of the Holy Spirit
in whom God may dwell.

But am I so as I read these words in the Office this early morning?
How I wish I could say so!
But my eyes I find closing.

And this prophecy from Zechariah in the same day's Office:
"The pots in the house of the Lord shall be as the libation bowls
before the altar. And every pot in Jerusalem and in Judah shall
be holy to the Lord of hosts" – does it not speak of the holiness
to which every soul is called, that every house shall become
as the temple of the Lord, and each of us a temple of His Spirit?
But how short do we fall of realizing His call, even now that
the Savior has come, even now that the Spirit is with us.
O let our house be a house of prayer!

(And I have just realized that it was only yesterday in our gospel
that zeal for the temple consumed our Lord and He declared (Lk.19:46):
"My house shall be a house of prayer" as He ejected the traders...
And on the readings of yesterday, this early morning I write a sentence.)

Let this house be built in the Lord's NAME!

Perhaps my Confession today will serve toward this purpose;
in it I spoke with the priest about prayer for at least fifteen minutes.
And I return home as if having received the Lord
in Holy Communion, able to taste Him in my mouth.
>   (And how good the food, the feast my wife has prepared,
>   is to my palate after two days of fasting.)

>   As the priest left the church I asked him of the soul
>   – re a writing I was correcting –
>   and its relation to God and ourselves...
>   And as I left, kneeling I lifted my head to the tabernacle
>> and saw how He must be first,
>> and how He must be all,
>> all I see and love;
>> for God is love,
>> and by Him and Him alone
>> we will love all He has made –
>> putting any love before Him
>> is not love at all.

>   Let me keep you ever before my eyes, O Lord!

A Conclusion

>   More and more time must I spend before the Lord
>   to help me remember His Presence,
>   to help me remember His NAME...
>   and a tabernacle I must find in my home
>   if this call is to be fulfilled.

IV. On Finding a House of Prayer

> "One thing I ask of the Lord;
> this I seek:
> To dwell in the Lord's house
> all the days of my life."
>
> Ps.27:4

2.

Striving

2/19/07

Like Jacob wrestling with the angel,
so all men must strive with God
to find the place reserved for them
here and in the kingdom.

Let us come into the New Israel –
here let us find a temple,
a House of Prayer.

IV. On Finding a House of Prayer

It is not easy, this striving with God,
but we are not alone in the fight:
we have the saints and angels
and the Blessed Mother
ever at our side.

And so why should we fear,
why question our call?
Let us but live it each day
and soon enough
we shall come to our Lord –
in His presence we will remain.

O Blessed Mother,
please remain close by,
guiding me along this way,
that I might be ever
on the path to the Lord,
never going astray.

Amen.

2. Striving

Here as I sit
in the presence of Christ
in Sacrament upon the altar,
here as I look upon
this white Host,
I wonder how I shall stay here.

I do not wish ever to leave
but to remain in His presence
always –
if His tabernacle
I am to become,
should I not know well
Him who is within me?

There is no other place
I would ever be
but here in His chapel.

But the Lord calls me forth
to be with my wife
and leads me to understand
that she will be
as my tabernacle.
Here I must learn
to make a home
while in this earthly wilderness.

And so, let me not be stubborn
or make my own way
but cherish obedience
to His voice.

And if I am to write,
even as I do here,
and if I am to publish
the works He inspires in me,
how can I stay
in this chapel long?
I must bring His light
to the world.

So this word as well
I must obey;
I must listen to His call,
for it would be vain
to do otherwise –
all must be in His will.

Yet a House of prayer
I would hope to find,
a temple to serve as a home.
Yes, I would be built
into His Church,
a living stone in Him,
founded firmly in His Body.

To this end, O Lord,
please lead me.

IV. On Finding a House of Prayer

2/20/07

Revelation 3:12
(from the Spirit's word
to the church in Philadelphia)

"He who conquers, I will make him a pillar in the temple of my God; never shall he go out of it, and I will write on him the name of my God, and the name of the city of my God, the new Jerusalem which comes down from my God out of heaven, and my own new name."

O let the promise of the Lord
   be fulfilled!
Let us be built into His House,
   His NAME upon us.

This is a book about
and of a process,
of finding a House of prayer.
As I begin I am not there,
by the time I end,
I hope to have entered within.

There is no greater call
than to become
a temple of the Lord,
to have His NAME
written on our souls –
to be as a tabernacle of God.
The House I hope to find
I pray will facilitate this,
but always, yes, the House
is within.

There is a certain call
to the diaconate this day –
in the illuminated, out of the way
greeting of an aging deacon,
in discussion with a servant
of the church
about the servant
a deacon is called to be,
and in a child
I haven't seen in years
asking me to baptize his son.
(All this in an hour's time.)

All this must be
in the Lord's hands,
in the way and time He pleases.

2. Striving

2/21/07
Ash Wednesday

It is Ash Wednesday, a day we remember especially our own mortality – that from dust we come and to dust we return – and I would like to relate a story of what I call my 'miracle flower', a white rose I gave (amongst a dozen) to my wife a few months ago, which is still in its place in a narrow vase before the Blessed Mother. After three weeks it remained virtually fresh and new, and though it has dried some, it is yet intact. [And remains so now, a year later.] One petal had bowed down (as if in prayer) and this was recently knocked off by my wife when she placed another flower in the same vase, but otherwise it remains whole. And the water level did not diminish for a good two months, till the placement of the other flower. [And has again remained steady for a number of months.]

Are we not called to be
as this flower?
Should we not ever endure?
Is it not God alone
who gives us life,
and what might shorten His hand?

I think of the saints
whose bodies remain incorrupt,
who even in flesh
have not returned to dust.

It is to eternal life we are called –
O Lord, may we be immortal
as you.

Of death
I have found myself afraid of late;
a certain doubt has on occasion
entered in.
I do not find myself ready,
or of sufficient faith.

As I find the childlike wonder
in speaking God's NAME
come closer to me,
even at this time, when I forget,
there is a tempting fear.

Only as a child will we enter
the kingdom –
simply be in God's presence.

IV. On Finding a House of Prayer

2/22/07
Chair of St. Peter

I have just finished reading
the Bible cover to cover
for the seventh time,
as ever, here before the Lord
exposed
in the Blessed Sacrament.

What glory awaits us,
brothers and sisters!

"Behold, the dwelling of God
is with men.
He will dwell with them,
and they shall be His people,
and God Himself will be
with them" (Rv.21:3).

Amen. Come, Lord Jesus.
Your Bride awaits,
to be made one with you
in heaven.

   It is Lent and I had been reading of what various persons are offering up this season, and had thought of what I might offer. My wife offered our walk to church this morning; a simple thing, it seemed... but during my Stations I realized: there is only one thing to be offered, and that is our very lives – everything we think, say, and do must be His.

O Lord, would you take
this offering of my life this season,
and keep it forever, I pray.
Let me hold nothing back
from you;
my weakness and my strength,
my spirit itself is yours.

The Father is hidden,
and we must be hidden with Him.
Though in the city of man,
though in the world we remain,
yet we must be present to Him
who is not seen
in the light of this day.

For in unending light He dwells,
away from the city's glare.
Let us kneel, brothers and sisters,
in His presence –
let us make our home there.

(Of Houses of prayer hidden
 as leaven in cities.)

We are nothing, nothing at all;
and so in Him we are strong.

(And the Lord shows me
 that everything is offered up
 in speaking His NAME.)

2. Striving

2/23/07

I thought yesterday
(and again today)
that only in the Church,
with our Mother's blessing,
will the House of prayer
be fulfilled –
only in her can it find a place
that is whole...
O that I might be a living stone
in this blessed Temple!

(On the founding of an order.)

O how beautifully
the golden-tongued saint
speaks of prayer this day
(in the Office of Readings):
"It is the longing for God,
love too deep for words,
a gift not given by man
but by God's grace."

Let us make our house
"a perfect dwelling place
for the Lord...
His image enthroned
in the temple of [our] spirit."

And I read my own writings
(here before
 the Sacrament exposed)
of the silence at the heart of all,
of the speaking
of the Divine NAME
in the world.

How to remember His silence,
which so quickly escapes me?
How to speak in His Word,
though so often distracted?

(O Jesus,
 please never let me leave.)

2/24/07

It is in the Cross.
It is in the Cross
the NAME of God is spoken,
the NAME of God is known,
for here the Word is spoken;
here in the sacrifice of Christ
our God reveals Himself.

It is not in this world,
not of this world...
it is in leaving this world,
laying down our lives,
we find Him who is Life.

IV. On Finding a House of Prayer

2/26/07

How shall we learn
not to be concerned
with ourselves;
how shall we learn
to live for God
and for others –
how shall we learn to love?

How shall we follow Jesus
along the narrow way
that alone leads to heaven?

O Lord, let me speak your NAME!

His flesh is the embodiment
of the NAME –
it is He who is Life,
who is Love,
who Is.

O Lord, how shall we be?
How shall we be with you
for all eternity,
we who are but dust?

(Let us be but dust
 and He will raise us up.)

The Blessed Mother has told me
I always have the key
to the tabernacle;
Jesus has said
I am His tabernacle...

The speaking of God's NAME
is the key to the tabernacle,
is that which leads
to making us His holy temple.

Open your mouth
and let the Spirit in,
in simplicity and in truth.
Remember His NAME
and remain in His presence
forever.

O but how poorly
I have remembered
His NAME!
How little I have spoken it
in these years.

It is remarkable, really:
a great gift the Lord gives me,
and I am blind to it,
failing in great measure
to appreciate this key.

Even in these days
as I seek to progress...
still I am forgetful,
and barely recollected.

2. Striving

But there is hope, I suppose.
There must be.
There must be possibility
that I will awaken,
cast off the human weakness,
the sin in which I'm lost,
and approach the Lord
as called.

Just to speak His NAME...
it seems a simple thing,
and it is.
A child make me before your face,
O holy Lord.

2/27/07

"Our Father..."

Remarkable it is, is it not,
that God would be called
our Father,
that us He would call His children?
Yet this is what we are!
If only we could come to realize it.

In this is love,
that the Father has sent
His only Son
that we might be returned
to our place as His children.

O Lord, let us call you "Father".

And it is the Holy Spirit
who brings light,
who opens our eyes
and leads us on right paths
to the Father of all.
What wisdom we need
to be as a child,
to be as the child Jesus is...
but the Spirit is at our side
to help us.

Call upon the Spirit.
Imitate the Son.
Find the Father living in you
and come thus to His kingdom.

O Mother,
through you let us come,
let us approach the Lord;
for then the way will be easy,
though wrought with many trials.

The suffering of the Son
let us embrace
with you ever standing nearby,
and straight to the Father
we shall come,
illumined by your Spouse's light.

"Father" let us call Him.
Father let Him be.
Children of the eternal God –
O Mother, let us join with thee!

IV. On Finding a House of Prayer

2/28/07

Was in the city, New York City, today, at the Church of St. Francis for Confession and Mass, and happened upon Exposition as well. It reminded me of *silence in the city*, a book I'd published and a truth I'd discovered – that even in the "noisiest" of places, God exists; God's NAME is spoken everywhere, if we could but listen.

If God is not here, where is He?
Where is He not?
It cannot but be that God is here,
here not just conceptually,
not just in our minds
if we think of Him...
but here, necessarily,
of His own will,
by His own nature –
He is everywhere,
if we could but see Him.
(He is more real than we
 or anything of this world.)

Oh but I am so forgetful!
I continue so blind and deaf,
so ignorant of His presence.
Why?
And how shall I find Him present
every day, at every hour,
every moment of my life?

He is near, my brother,
here, where you sit or stand;
there is no escaping His presence
except by our ignorance,
poor souls that we are.

3/1/07

Is there nothing for us to do?
Are all our efforts useless?
It is true, grace and love
come from God
and this is what sustains us,
what saves us...
but are we to do nothing at all?
Yes, acceptance is key,
laying down our lives before Him...
but even a child
must serve his parents.
And so the Lord calls us
to answer His love,
to receive His grace,
and with this build our lives,
build His kingdom on this earth.

2. Striving

We are creatures made to work,
made to do,
to do the will of the Lord
and cultivate His earth.
And so,
indeed with anxious concern
let us work out our salvation,
even as His Rock has instructed;
there is no place for complacency
in God's Church –
or do you think His kingdom
is already complete?
Eyes of faith and love
see otherwise,
and to our hearts our Savior calls,
to do His work in this world.

And the crowning work of man
Is prayer;
it is the food of His saints.
Nothing is more efficacious
than this,
nothing more powerful.
Call upon His NAME, my friend;
beg His will be done.
Then you shall find indeed
He does all things,
and we are but poor servants.
Instruments of His light,
soldiers of His peace...
by grace we become
as Jesus Himself,
His Body on this plane.
For this gift you must pray to God.

3/2/07

Light in the eyes,
Light in the mind,
Light of the Holy Spirit...
Wisdom from on high
we need to guide our days –
I need Him here
to write these words
upon this page.

If the Holy Spirit be not with us,
truly we are lost,
lost in the darkness
where heaven cannot shine.

But with Him
heaven indeed we approach
and serve to build up on this earth;
His light to the tips of our fingers,
within us our God reigns.

As I sit again before the Lord
exposed upon the altar
(as I do each page of this book),
the light of the Spirit
I find filling my mind,
my eyes alight with His flame.
(How greatly He holds us
 in His arms;
 with what love the Spirit comes.)

IV. On Finding a House of Prayer

And I cannot say (who can say?)
that He inspires
each of these lines,
but this indeed is my hope,
that He accepts
this offering of mine.

And more than this I pray He take,
O Spirit who is as Light;
all my ways and all my days
I pray be blessed
with His holy life.

Without you I stumble blindly,
Spirit God divine.
Be near me with your blessings;
your grace and wisdom
be my guide.

3/5/07

At this time I am renewing my consecration to Jesus through Mary as prescribed by St. Louis de Montfort, following the recommended time and readings more closely and fully than in recent years.

Today I begin the first week, pertaining to knowledge of one's self, a knowledge that can but tell us we are nothing, nothing but sinners – for this is the truth before God. (Only by His grace and mercy are we made anything at all.)

As I have struggled to remember God's NAME, so I have struggled to remember and live my consecration to the Lord through His Blessed Mother's intercession. There was a time her guidance was close at hand, close as my heartbeat... but now so little do I think of the blessing of her presence.

She will take us directly to God; this we must know, brothers and sisters, for with the Lord – Father, Son, and Holy Spirit – she is intimately acquainted. There is no other soul joined to Him as is she; by her we will come to union with God.

In the scapular I wear (and also neglect) Mary holds Jesus' Cross in place (at the back through the letters INRI), and so the scapular as a whole to me. All our connection to the Lord, His very arms around our shoulders, would fall quickly from us were she not to maintain His blessing.

And so I pray
I shall better call upon her,
better seek her intercession,
that by such grace I may come
to better remember
the Lord's NAME,
and so His presence.

2. Striving

3/6/07

O sweet humility
and patience come from Christ...
a certain purgatorial darkness
upon our souls
is necessary to find the light.

Nothing kills the spirit more surely
than the pride of man,
a pride akin to the devil's own,
which can but separate us
from God's hand.

(There is great refreshment
 in silently bowing
 before His throne.)

And how can wisdom exist
without love?
For it would then be wickedness.
(As without wisdom,
 love would turn to lust.)

A compassionate heart we need,
and this never forget;
for if we fail ever to forgive,
we will but find God's judgment
ourselves.

(A gentle heart fans the flames
 of the mind
 in accord with the Spirit's grace.)

O break my pride, dearest Lord,
that your love might be my own,
that I might live in innocence
as a child before your throne.

Else I can but flee in fear
for the sin upon my soul;
else I shall surely die
when your light becomes known.

Save me, Lord, from myself,
from the vanity all about;
brought to life by my blindness,
it is dispelled by a word
from your mouth.

3/7/07

I have repeatedly made note of my failure to remember the Lord's NAME, but have not put forth here other failures in prayer.

In particular, my Rosary is often vain, spoken without thought, mechanically. Though, as with speaking the NAME, I know what I should do – I have been given a method of breathing the verses in meditation and contemplation... I do not take the time I should; and so my prayer is indeed quite empty.

IV. On Finding a House of Prayer

3/8/07

My Liturgy of the Hours
also often falls short
of recollected chanting
in the Spirit of the Lord…

And I have had to pray
the Divine Mercy Chaplet
in my extra hour
before the Sacrament,
or it would be neglected, too.
Though I strive to wake
more strictly at 2 a.m.,
many of my hours are not held to
with the discipline prescribed.

And I do not pray with my wife
as I should,
failing also in prayer shared…
and now she is going away
for two weeks,
when no occasion for this union
will be here.

We do consider seriously
a call to celibate life,
hoping this will be a holy offering
made unto the Lord…
but we must join
our hearts and minds
in prayer unto God,
or of what use will be
this marriage;
what fruit will there be in our lives?

I am reading
Turn of the Jubilee Year,
account of my vocation search
made to several monasteries
nearly seven years ago…
I am hoping it will serve
to help me find spiritual direction.

It is remarkable how provident
the entries and occurrences were
at the time of writing,
particularly for
Five Days in the Desert –
all readings and practices
seem to coincide
in the will of God.

I see that many things
I struggled with then,
I struggle with now…
but that with a little application
and remembrance (and fortitude)
the difficulties can be overcome…
and the way of the Lord found
in my life.

Last night I thought to eat,
to break my bread fast
for Wednesday,
hungry and with a headache
and fearing this weakness…
but I did not eat
and found strength last night
and into this morning.

2. Striving

All can be done in Christ.
And with His light we see
that He is in all things.

The coincidences
strike again today:
today's gospel appears
in my Bible reading
toward consecration.
It is of the rich man and Lazarus.

O Lord, make me poor
as Francis himself,
in whose church I now sit.
Let me be nothing but a beggar
for the poor,
for the salvation of souls.

3/9/07

By performing the opposite virtue,
vices may be rooted out.
This is a simple truth
of the spiritual life,
and one which I finally
come to understand.

A call to pray
for the salvation of all
is upon my soul.
I have heard it before,
but now it becomes clearer.
And would this practice not serve
to conquer the judgmental attitude
so much a bane
to my spiritual progress –
would it not mean loving all?

As I pray the Sorrowful Mysteries
for the people surrounding me
on the subway train,
so let me remember to pray for all,
for their salvation;
for no greater love can there be
and no quicker way
to defeat the devil.

But to remembering this,
to practicing it,
along with rejoicing in suffering
with the Lord –
which would counteract
a complaining tongue –
I must do…
I must consistently apply myself.

Work harder when lazy;
carry the Cross –
only in this will you find freedom…
Only in this is God's peace.

But, above all,
what a joy it would be
to pray for the salvation
of every soul,
every single person
we meet or see,
all we even think of.
Here is the heart
of the order I find;
here a call to lay down one's life
that others might be raised.
(No sweeter drink is there
in this world
than the Lord's holy blood.)

IV. On Finding a House of Prayer

3/12/07

Yet the heart of hearts,
the spirit and soul of the order
and of every Christian life,
is God's Divine NAME –
speaking His silence
and being in His presence,
remaining there always
at the heart of our hearts
where the Father dwells
in peace
beyond our understanding,
in light
beyond our comprehension.
Here we must make our home;
this is our call.

The Father and the Son (and the Spirit) are one, inseparably one; and wherever the Father is, there is the Son; and wherever the Son is, there is the Father... here is unbreakable unity of Being. Yet the Father is greater than the Son, as the Son Himself has told us; and though God's NAME and His Cross are inseparable as Father and Son, and one is not had without the other, the Father and His surpassing peace we poor humans put in the first place.

Let the Cross reveal
the NAME of God,
His eternal presence among us,
just as the Son reveals the Father
and His undying love.
We do not know the Father
except by the Son,
and we do not know His NAME,
we do not come into
the Father's presence,
except by the Cross of the Christ.
Carry it we must to be bereft of all
that keeps us from the Father
in this world;
emptied of ourselves we shall find
the life of God within us.

3/13/07

And the Holy Spirit
and His Promise,
His light and His hope,
cannot, of course, be separated
from the Life of God
and His Cross;
indeed He brings us both,
and brings both to fulfillment
in us,
even as He has done
in the Blessed Mother.

O fire of the Holy Spirit,
may the Father's will
be accomplished in us
by the Cross of Jesus,
and by your power.

2. Striving
3/15/07

O Blessed Mother,
all graces come through you
by the power of your Spouse,
the Spirit.
Pray we shall receive all the grace
the Lord would ordain
be ours.
Open our hearts
to accept His Word
as gratefully and readily
as you, dear Mother.
May we be worthy to be called
your children,
cast in your holy image,
in the image of your divine Son.
Pray we too conceive by the Spirit,
and bring Jesus to the world.

How wonderfully the saint (Louis de Montfort) speaks of the blessings upon Mary and her necessity to our salvation. It is she through whom we come to God, even as He has come to us through her. And we are all formed in her womb with Jesus.

And I see that the Spirit is Mary's Spouse, that it is He who conceives the Son in her, and so indeed must, too, be called male, as the Father and the Son. (There is a marvelous balance, a perfect complementarity, to God and His Church.)

The sweetness of Mary
how can any of us approach;
how can any of us know
her beauty, her sweet fragrance,
her perfect purity...
for would we not
in approaching her
spoil that perfection
she has as a gift from God?
How can our souls bear
such loveliness?
O Mother, pray for us,
and place your arms around us,
that we might
by the grace you bear
come to know the Lord our God.

It is only through her
we come to him;
only through her sweet perfection
do we taste the perfection
only God possesses...
only by her
are we united with Him.
O Lord, this path you leave us,
this way you lead us on –
this Virgin we could never imagine
to ask for,
this grace no other way
would we know,
except that you provide her to us.
May we come freely to her
whom you give,
that we may know you fully
in our lives.

IV. On Finding a House of Prayer

And she is Mother of the Church,
through whom salvation comes.
She gives birth to His brothers
even as she has to her Son;
and the Spirit upon her
and her Son
is with these brothers,
these apostles,
to lead the Bride to her Groom.
And we shall be wed in heaven
to our Lord and God,
to Him whom she is already wed,
the first to enter His kingdom;
and so it is she who leads us
upon this nuptial path
she has trod
to our eternal God.

3/16/07

Be consecrated to our Lady,
and so to our Blessed Lord;
it cannot but be
that the One follows the other.
For He is her Son,
having given life to Him,
and so to us, dear brothers.

Let her give life to you as well.
Hesitate not to give yourself
to her,
and she will give you to the Lord
who gives life to all.
Find life here in your Mother.

In this order dedicated
to the Father
one must have devotion
to the Blessed Mother,
or be a bastard son.
What good son is there
that does not honor his mother?
What father would be pleased
to see a mother disdained?
And would you dishonor
the Father of all
by failing to devote yourself
to the Mother
He has ordained for His Son
and for all His brothers?
Give the greater honor
to this Blessed Mother
in whose debt you are eternally.

And separate yourself not
from the Church,
even in the least matter;
obedience treasure in all things.
For this Mother speaks for you,
cares for you,
would teach and feed you well
on your journey here –
this, too, the Father ordains.
Though there be no priest
without sin,
though no man be perfect
but Him whom we adore,
yet He is in His Church
with His Spirit to direct,
and so perfection is present
herein.

3/19/07

Variations. There are variations, possible changes... should I make a firmer plan? If I weren't to walk to Mass, I couldn't say my Rosaries then; perhaps they should be scheduled more objectively.

And doesn't it make sense to simplify and state a Rosary in a particular position: say, Joyful seated, Luminous walking (always aft.?), Sorrowful kneeling, Glorious standing (or lying down... and perhaps in the Vigil hour...)? Would this move toward standardization be wise?

If I think to leave a form for others, an order to follow – that may best be fulfilled after I'm gone – then perhaps it should take a definite shape, not predicated on my situation. Perhaps I could even note my own adaptation of the norm... and thereby my own variations. I have always loved the Trappist discipline, their adherence to the hours. There is, I believe, great freedom there. And so a definite form, a clearer horarium, becomes a thought. (And is this order somehow especially for writers?)

O blessed St. Joseph,
builder of the house of God,
pray the Lord build the temple for me,
that I not labor in vain.
I would honor the Father
with this work dedicated to Him
and to His hidden presence...
Foster-father of Jesus,
pray it shall be acceptable;
let His will be done in me
as it has in you.
O that I might be a just instrument
as you, O father,
have proved to be.

There seem to be three kinds of orders: contemplative, mendicant, and didactic, and the three seem to relate to the three Persons of the Trinity: Father, Son, and Holy Spirit. (There are also secular societies that do the work of the Church.)

(If writing is the contemplative art,
done most in solitude,
perhaps this is why I wonder
if this order is for such as these.)

IV. On Finding a House of Prayer

But all must have devotion to all three Persons – as the Three are inseparable and all must be with each – though perhaps with a particular orientation. As with this order characterized by the Father: prayer is most important, but that prayer must extend to others; it must serve them (as it does in concern for souls' salvation). And the teaching must also be accomplished, though here only in books and not so directly as in classrooms... as the service of the poor is not lifting bodies from the streets, but from the spiritual pits.

3/20/07

Prayer, service to the poor,
and the preaching of the Word...
these three indeed
seem to sum up
the call upon our souls
in accord with the Persons
of the Most Holy Trinity.

Three is always the number
of divinity,
and adding another
we enter and make it human...
four is the number of the universe,
of the world of man.
We the Church
round out the Trinity
and become thus one with God.

The soul, the heart, and the mind
are here in these three calls –
let us perform them
with all our strength
and be one and whole
and complete
in the Body of Christ our Lord.

Here in the silence of prayer
we make our principal home;
the Father
(He who is hidden from our sight),
is always first in this order,
in this way.
Let Him write His NAME
upon your soul.

Founded in the Presence
of the Father,
we can reach out to our neighbor
as Jesus, in love,
here, as I say,
by prayer for his soul's salvation;
but in many ways
let our neighbor be fed.
Fed also with the Spirit
he must be,
with the Father's light,
for he must find his way along
lighted paths...
and so let him be taught,
let God's Word
be preached to him,
that his way may be clear
and free of error, free of sin,
and founded in
the House of the Lord.

2. Striving

3/21/07

Where one Person is,
the others are, always;
and so we should never play
one against another
or be ignorant of any
but allow them always
to serve the others
in our meditation.
And Mary, too,
even Mary is fruitful
in bringing us to the Persons
of the Most Holy Trinity –
for she is one with them
as we are called to be.

We should always try
to remember
the other Persons
when concentrating on any one.
For instance, in my Stations
I find myself thinking
only of Jesus…
but then something is missing,
even of Jesus –
there is a lack of wholeness
to our thoughts.
Never think the others
(or even Mary)
will distract from one or another;
know they will but fulfill each other
in your thoughts and in fact.

And Mary, yes, Mary…
she can but bring us closer
to each Person of the Trinity.
Sometimes when I contemplate
the Father,
when I seek to speak His NAME,
I can think that here
Mary has no place…
as invisible as the Father is.
But her visibility,
her concrete presence,
as well as that of the Church,
is no distraction
but, again, fulfillment,
a sure guide to the Father's reign.
(The imageless is not demeaned
 by she who is made
 in His image.)

3/22/07

And I see, too, that marriage
is no hindrance to union with God,
to remaining present to the Trinity
through the intercession of Mary,
but also may be a help,
a means of drawing closer
to the Lord;
for is it not in this sacrament
that we know unity of persons,
a unity of persons
like that known so perfectly
in the Most Holy Trinity?
And so this sacrament
can indeed be a great blessing
for the spiritual life.

IV. On Finding a House of Prayer

3/23/07

My wife has returned
from two weeks away
and things seem to have changed;
things seem much better
in our marriage,
perhaps because they are better
in ourselves.
The idea of being celibate
passes now
and the sacramental act
seems to find fruit,
a fruit of unity of persons in love.
A great gift
the Lord offers me again;
I pray I now accept it well
and live according to His word
and way.

For my own part,
an anger has subsided...
a fear perhaps at its source
is fading.
It may be remembering to pray
for all souls
and their salvation,
but the trial of the past two weeks
seems to be bearing the fruit
of a spiritual progress.
I pray it take root
and grow unto heaven.

How do we give ourselves
entirely to the Lord,
as He desires
(and as we should desire,
 if we have any sense,
 any love in our hearts)?
How do we renounce ourselves
and join Him upon the Cross,
knowing the freedom that is found
only there?
Let us pray He will guide us
to this place
by the power of the Holy Spirit
and the intercession
of His Blessed Mother.

The holy man (de Kempis)
speaks of doing this
in Holy Communion,
of each day offering ourselves
with Him
in the Sacrament of the altar.
And the saint (de Montfort)
speaks of doing this
through union with Mary,
the perfect mold and model
of life in Christ.
Let us do both,
and with ardor,
and with remembrance.

2. Striving

O dear, sweet Jesus,
how wonderful it would be
to be united completely with you,
and so with your Father
and the Holy Spirit.
If we could but give up our lives
as you request,
as you wish for us
that we might be blessed,
how happy indeed we would be.
Let us share in your love,
your surpassing, undying love –
no more could we ask or need.
Let it be so, dear Lord, let it be so.
Overtake our souls this day.

3/26/07

It's a beautiful day,
a wonderful day –
the Annunciation,
a day for the renewal
of consecration to Jesus
through Mary.
Confession and communion
and special prayer...
and again a call to pray
for all souls:
"Pray for everyone,"
Mary says to me
as I walk down
these New York City streets.

Here is the hermit in the city,
quietly, within himself,
looking upon the faces
of all who pass by,
of all around
(and even in the buildings)...
and praying for them,
offering them to the Lord.
"In every place you are,"
she reminds me,
as I enter the restaurant.
Everywhere, everyone...
pray for all, without fail,
without judgment.

Yes, she is the means
to union with God,
the Father, Son, and Holy Spirit
(she who is so united to them).
Yes, in speaking God's NAME
we offer ourselves
entirely to Him.
Yes, let us give our hands
and our feet,
let us offer ourselves completely
to the Lord
and in obedience
follow in His way,
according to His command...
even as our Blessed Mother.

IV. On Finding a House of Prayer

3/27/07

On this day after the Annunciation,
I begin reading
Pope John Paul II's
Theology of the Body.
It is confirmed in the first few
introductory pages
what was presented
in a book on the Trinity
I finished today:
that man and woman participate
in the Trinitarian life,
in particular through marriage
and the marital act –
the two becoming one.
Here they come to know
and to be like God,
Father, Son, and Holy Spirit.

In Mary this Trinitarian life
is most fully known and fulfilled
among us creatures –
she being in perfect union
with Father, Son, and Spirit
(a union clearly not dependent
 upon the sexual act
 for its discovery…).
We aspire to her blessed state
and, it is fresh in my mind today,
may attain such union,
such holiness,
by her intercession.

People place their money in a bank for its safekeeping and its growth. It is not with them; they do not carry it on their persons, but it is present in this separate place, this useful institution.

And is not Mary the bank for all our spiritual lives, yes, all our lives? Should we not place all our prayers, all our thoughts and words and deeds, and even Jesus Himself, in her hands and in her heart, that they might be protected and grow?

(O Safe Harbor, take all that I am for the Lord.)

3/28/07

The Lord is before me again.
What shall I say?
There is nothing to be said
here in the place of silence…

but on I must go.

I love you, Lord.
(Here let me stay.)

2. Striving

3/30/07

Children. Children of light,
the light of God,
the love of God...
this is what we're called
to become:
to shed all darkness,
all sin,
and come innocently
and humbly,
truthfully, sincerely,
before our God
as His children,
giving to Him all
He has given to us.

St. Anthony holds the baby Jesus
in his arms
so tenderly,
so gently...
and he would place Him
in our heart.
And if we would hold Him there,
we would be whole,
we would be happy –
we would be of light,
with no darkness in us.
(Let such holy innocence,
 such purity,
 be our salvation.)

There are many images
to describe our relationship
with the Lord,
many qualities
and many ages of man...
but the child is the truest age
and the truest image.
We have a heart, mind,
soul, and body,
but it is our spirit
that is closest to Him,
to our God.
Here let us find ourselves
in innocence,
as a child before God.

4/2/07

Can we be poor
yet possess things?
Can we be disciples of Christ
if we do not give up all we own?
This question comes to mind
at Mass this morning.
Do we not begin
to become disciples
when we sell everything
and give it to the poor,
that we might have
nothing else to give
but God?
While we yet own things,
are we not necessarily
attached to them –
do they not yet wait
to be given away?

231

IV. On Finding a House of Prayer

4/3/07

The gospel was
of Judas' complaint
that the poor could have been fed
if Mary's perfume had been sold.
I realized Jesus never really
fed the poor;
when once (or twice)
He multiplied the loaves,
He rebuked the masses
for returning to Him seeking food.
And Peter says to the cripple
at the gate of the temple:
"I have no silver and gold,
but I give you what I have;
in the name of Jesus Christ
of Nazareth, walk" (Acts 3:6).

If we have nothing,
we have no further need
to consider Matthew 25 –
we will have no goods
to give to the poor...
they will have all been given.
Then we may begin to give
the food Jesus truly came
to deliver:
then we can proclaim
the Word of God
and heal all those who come to us
in His name.
(Again I ask,
 can we be His disciples
 and yet own things –
 will our ministry
 not be incomplete...
 is detachment really possible
 while yet possessing?)

Though religious poverty
may indeed be the ideal,
it does not seem to be my call
as a hermit in the city.
Even after writing
yesterday's entry,
as I prayed to the Blessed Mother
she reminded me
of what she had said
in our locutions several years ago:
that she is not calling me
to give up work
or other things of this world
(which now would include
 marriage),
but to transcend them
even as I am participating in them.

I can discern two purposes
to this call:
first, for myself
it would be purgatorial,
a challenge, a discipline,
to remember the presence of God
even in the midst of distractions.
Here great refinement of faith
may be found.
Second, for others
it may serve as witness
that the Lord can meet a soul
wherever he may be.
This purpose is thus incarnational,
bringing the Lord to the world...
much as Jesus has come
into our midst.

2. Striving

So, "in the city" it seems
I must stay –
in an urban environment,
yes, perhaps,
and working at a college,
using a computer, etc....
But what is most upon my soul
at this time
is making a home with my wife,
becoming one with her.
Peace within ourselves
must be first,
but other places requiring peace
soon follow.
So let us not struggle against
the places and the people
the Lord brings into our days –
but make His home there.

4/4/07

Union with the divine will
is, of course, always the goal
of the spiritual life,
is always man's great desire
and only fulfillment,
and coincides, necessarily,
with the desire of God.
It is His will He would have us
freely embrace,
that we might be joined to Him
who has created us all.
Let us be as His only Son.

Only Jesus is our Redeemer.
He takes upon Himself
our poor flesh,
enters our pitiable state,
but to raise us up
from such pitiable condition.
We are weak,
we are dead and dying,
our bodies fading day to day...
but here is the Lord!
He unites us to God
as He unites Himself to us –
and so the Father's loving will
may be done
and we be one with Him.

See your weak flesh, my friend.
Notice how limited you are –
but a creature, a human being,
always of the earth.
God is far above you
and your ways.
Do you not see that you would die
with this passing world
if not for Jesus,
if not for the Father's love...
if not for the illumination
that comes by the Spirit?
Let Him lift you from the ground
to walk with Him.

IV. On Finding a House of Prayer

4/5/07
Holy Thursday

In silence, all is spoken.

Lay down your life for others,
for their salvation,
as Jesus has done.

O Lord, give light to my eyes
(and let me find my place
 in the Body of Christ).

4/9/07
Easter Monday

The Lord is risen!
Alleluia!

And by His resurrection
draws us unto the kingdom
where He reigns –
O how He would have us be
His humble subjects!
O how His Spirit would serve
to seat us at table with Him!
Let us be before Him always
as His blessed children –
to holy innocence let us return.

How happy I am
to be here before the Lord again.
How happy to bask
in the light of this season,
of this Easter Day.

And how happy to begin now
the Theology of the Body proper;
the great Pope's words
I start to read this day
(after finishing Thursday
 the book's lengthy introduction).

And in the first few pages
(discussing "the beginning"),
the Holy Father states
that Genesis 1 and Exodus 3
(the two biblical texts –
 along with 1Kings 3 –
 I have primarily quoted
 in discussion of the divine NAME)
have become "the source
of the deepest inspirations
for the thinkers
who have sought to understand
'being' and 'existing'" (#2,9/12/79).

I cannot help but wonder
what I may be learning
from the Lord
quite ingenuously.

2. Striving

4/10/07
Easter Tuesday

Does not man's greatest gift
consist in his call to prayer,
to worship God?
Yes, he is distinguished by love,
is made to love,
as no other creature;
and yes he is created to make,
to subdue, to build,
to use his hands
to form and utilize
objects of the earth,
to till the ground...
but is not his greatest call
to prayer?

Man was made to worship God,
to know the joy of His Creator
by entering into His presence,
into His love,
and he can only be fulfilled
by answering
this call from the Lord
wrought into his very being.
All the earth does praise the Lord,
but only man
becomes as God Himself.
(May the Light of the Spirit
 infuse our souls.)

And Jesus, of course,
this God made Man,
is He who returns us
to the divine image,
to the divine presence;
born amongst us and dying for us,
He raises us to eternal life
as He rises from the grave.
On this Easter day let Him work,
let His grace fill you.
You have done your work
during Lent,
you have tried to die to self
but found
you were only able to kill the Lord.
Yes, now it is His time to work,
to answer your feeble prayers.

4/11/07
Easter Wednesday

Reading John Paul II's discourse on man and woman, husband and wife, as the original communion of persons (and on their being a reflection of God), I cannot but wonder at its significance for the formation of an "order", a community, based on marriage. If marriage is the original communion, would it not also be the ideal communion today?

(Seems to lend credence to idea
 of a married hermit in the city.)

IV. On Finding a House of Prayer

4/12/07
Easter Thursday

I have spoken before
of Sylvia and I
joining so thoroughly,
in particular in prayer,
that we become as one pray-er,
as one person
in worship of God.
How would our marriage,
our conjugal union,
affect this unity?
Would it not add to this oneness,
enriching, if not fulfilling it?

Let me pray,
through the intercession
of John Paul the Great,
for direction and guidance,
for light from the Holy Spirit,
regarding my marriage
and this order.
Let both (as one) be offered
to the Lord
as incense before His throne,
and through them
His NAME be known.

Yesterday in praying the Divine Mercy Chaplet with my wife before the exposed Blessed Sacrament at 3:00, a further understanding of the Divine NAME came to me. Instead of advancing to the next bead immediately after speaking my part (leading the prayer), which had become my habit with this prayer and the Rosary, I listened first to my wife complete her half of the prayer. In this short moment of time, I found blessed opportunity to speak God's silent NAME (rather than simply waiting for my wife to finish).

I thought again of how little time
it takes to speak God's NAME,
and realized further
that this NAME and its speaking
is not tied to time,
as it is beyond
and at the heart of time,
and so –
as I remembered that it is
at the heart of all words,
of all true speech (and sound) –
that it can be spoken, in a sense,
outside time,
always,
eternally...
(as it should be).

2. Striving

And so the simple practice
of waiting till a prayer
is ended
before advancing to the next bead
leads in this instance
and may serve generally
(again, in Chaplet
 as well as Rosary)
as a means
of better remembering
the NAME of God,
of deepening one's prayer life
and furthering union with the Lord.

As I speak God's NAME
this early morning,
as I offer Him my thoughts,
asking, begging
that they be of Him,
His gaze, His breath,
penetrates my head;
and can I help but cry,
but moan in pain,
though the pain be beautiful?
My thoughts are not His thoughts,
are very far, particularly far,
from His.
O Father, please take
this innermost part of me,
and make it your own!

4/13/07
Easter Friday

And of the Father and His NAME,
of Him who is hidden and secret
and of His silence...
and of His penetrating gaze,
wherein we discover
our nakedness:
John Paul II speaks
of man's original nakedness
and relates it to the vision of God,
which sees all things.
In his original innocence,
man was not ashamed –
He could stand before
the eye of the Lord.
(Upon his fall,
 He could do so no more.)

And as my thoughts and prayers
are not with the Father,
my words are not with the Son;
they do not call
for men's salvation,
but tend rather to speak
in judgment of them.
And this realization brings
pervasive tears,
despite this Easter day.
(O Lord, help me to love!)

And how wise are my actions,
how led by the Spirit am I?
And in His Church,
at His Mother's side,
do I find my strength?
I am too much apart from God!

IV. On Finding a House of Prayer

4/14/07
Easter Saturday

Nothing. To be nothing
before God.
I return to this... joy,
to this deep, abiding, liberating
humility –
if we are nothing, truly nothing,
(save perhaps an instrument,
 a pen in God's hand),
then God is everything,
as He is, in truth.
Let us not know ourselves,
but God;
let us cast off our pride,
and let Him enter
and make His home in us.

How this state is attained
I cannot say, brothers and sisters,
for it is the work of the Holy Spirit.
But let us have faith,
let us increase in faith,
and truly, let us be nothing,
nothing before God.
Let us humble ourselves
under His mighty hand
and He will lift us up
unto His kingdom,
be assured.
O Lord, let me be nothing,
hold nothing,
before you!

We must be tabernacles of God,
His holy dwelling place
on this earth.
The Holy Father speaks of man's
original innocence,
of the holiness of his person
(even his very body)
before the Fall...
and it is to this state
we must return.
By the grace of the Lord
this original grace may be found,
may be reborn in us.
And we can become holy again
by the sacrifice of Jesus.

4/16/07

Forgiveness.
How do we find forgiveness?
How can we be forgiven,
we who have done
so much wrong?

It does not seem possible.
Humanly, it is not.
And so we need the Christ;
and so we need the grace
of the Lord.

2. Striving
4/17/07

Does His resurrection not teach us
precisely of forgiveness?
Does it not show that
all the sins we have brought
against Him
to crucify Him
have been turned back,
have themselves been destroyed?
Is it not His first act (after rising)
to grant His disciples
power to forgive men's sins?
Is this not Jesus' whole purpose,
His very reason
for coming among us –
that we might be saved,
that we might be washed clean?

And so, to be forgiven
we must have faith
in His resurrection.
We must believe
that the same Jesus
who was so cruelly tortured
unto death
on Good Friday
is now risen from the grave
we made as His home.

Faith in the resurrection
is everything.
It is not easy,
and to it we are often blind,
but it is this faith
we must most nourish
here and through all our time.

The Lord is risen, alleluia!
(O that we would never forget;
upon such remembrance
our salvation rests.)

I would like to discuss further understanding of the three divine Persons (and Mary, and the Church, the Body of Christ) as it seems to gain clarity. Generally, it seems (though a case could be made for each in the place of the others) our thoughts are related to the Father, our words to the Son, and our actions to the Spirit (and the Church).

The Father is indeed hidden and secret, the deepest, most profound Person, the Creator of all, source of all, whom no man can see or understand. And are not our thoughts of the innermost man, the deepest, most subtle part of us, by which we are moved? And should they not be given to the Father? (O what freedom one should then know!)

The Son is the spoken Word, come for our salvation, our redemption... and should not all our words desire only the salvation of souls – should we not speak His word, walk in His steps?

IV. On Finding a House of Prayer

And the Spirit gives us light,
leads us and guides us,
counseling us into all truth;
wisdom is ours in Him. And so
should He not guide our actions?
Should all we do not be directed
by the Spirit?

And do not our actions find
great strength in union with His
Bride, His Church, by the
intercession of our Blessed
Mother, the Spirit's holy Spouse?
Here in this Body of Christ we find
the fullness of our call as sons and
daughters of God realized and
made strong.

4/18/07

It seems to me the Christian life
in this age
is like praying
the Stations of the Cross
during Easter Season.

I had thought
perhaps I should refrain
from praying the Stations
for the remainder of Easter,
as I had for the Octave
(and as I do all Sundays
 and Solemnities)...
but the Blessed Mother
indicates to me
the grace this practice can be
even in this time of joy.

We are living now
under the resurrection,
for Christ has been raised
and He shall never die again.
So our season now is Easter.
But yet we carry the Cross
in this world,
for yet the world
and we ourselves
are subject to sin
and in need of penance.
Every day we must
take up our cross.
And so, though walking
the way of sorrow
with our saving Lord,
ever we should have joy
in our souls,
knowing that through all suffering
we shall come to His eternal glory.

Before the coming of the Lord
they lived as though
singing canticles
in a time of Lent,
for though without the Christ
and so as walking in a desert,
yet they kept their hope alive
that the promise would be fulfilled.
Now He has come;
now new life is upon us...
but now we are more aware, too,
that we are yet travelers here,
having not entered fully
into heaven.

2. Striving

4/19/07

"This night your soul
is required of you" (Lk.12:20).

This parable of the rich 'fool', from which this quote is taken, is usually interpreted as a warning against storing up earthly possessions. But, though the message regarding greed is certainly there, I see the parable more as a warning against sloth, noticing more so the man's words about taking his ease. And it seems that a lesson against complacency may be even more needed in this day and among the well-off of the first world.

Is it not the desire to have nothing to do, no work to accomplish, that drives even the amassing of goods? Is it not this wanting to take our ease that plagues so many hearts and souls? Not realizing or accepting that only in heaven will we find reward, will the Lord serve us at table, we work night and day (and/or play the lottery) anxious but to retire. But we must learn that – put in colloquial terms – "there is no vacation from our vocation", or suffer ever mental distress.

The Lord is ever calling us; every night it is as if we die and must make account for that day. Every day we must do His will, every moment recognize His presence, for nothing done in the past will save our souls this day; and if ever we turn from the Lord, we shall lose our way.

It is a great blessing,
this call in our souls –
it is God's love inviting us
to greater progress,
closer union with Him.
Let us not fear
but embrace the cross
He so gently bears to us this day.

4/21/07

Time is short.
Death is near, always,
and the end of the world
is at hand.
And so, should we not remember
the NAME of the Lord?
What else matters?
Why are we so distracted?
Why do other things
seem more important than God?
All time is in the heart of Christ,
and He will take care…
and yet we fret.
Why not trust in Him?
Would this not be
the wisest thing?

IV. On Finding a House of Prayer

4/23/07

I come to prayer
in the middle of the night
and still find it difficult
to sit in silence,
to speak with the Lord.
Though it is the simplest thing
and requires no time at all,
yet I cannot seem to come to Him.
Why? Is He not there,
is He not waiting?
Of course He is,
but where am I?
My mind is on a hundred things,
none of which compares to Him,
and none of which
He couldn't care for –
why don't I give Him His time?

Be not afraid.
It is I, says the Lord.
And He but loves us
and holds all our time in His heart.
It takes but a moment
to come into His presence.
(He smiles at me
 as I realize this,
 as I realize the foolishness
 of my failing to recognize Him.)
In but that moment
your prayer can be well prepared,
well-given to the Lord,
that He might bless it and you.
Trust in Him,
and you will see Him work.
(Always remember His NAME.)

How does one rejoice in suffering?
How does one find
the blessing it can be
when united with Christ's own?
By uniting it with Christ's own.

If we suffer apart from Him,
we suffer vainly.
If we suffer with the Lord,
how blessed indeed are we!

There is no greater joy
than to be united
with Christ's Cross,
which is our ladder to heaven.

In the Cross is the greatest joy,
but how do we find the Cross?
How do we make Jesus, God,
the center of our lives?
By giving everything over to Him
and trusting in His wisdom.

Yet certainly it can be difficult
to remember all is His:
easily possessiveness
can creep in
and overtake our thinking.
Sometimes it is as if
we are in a dark room
unable to find His breath, the light,
unable to give our thoughts
to Him.
Let us not cease the struggle
to remember His NAME.

And how easily we fall
into judgment,
how quickly we forget to pray
for the salvation of all souls.
It gives us freedom
when we remember –
let us make it part of our days.

Closer we can only hope to draw,
casting the devil's illusions aside.
More greatly blessed
we can only hope to be,
knowing this is the will of Him
who created us for His love.

May our mouths not cease
to utter praise
for all the Lord does in our lives.

4/24/07

There seem to be two mistakes we consistently make in the spiritual life. First, we think we can do something, if not all things; second, we think God is unable to do anything. The truth is exactly the opposite, of course: God can do all things; we can do nothing... and so how often the Lord must break our pride to teach us of His way, to show it is only in Him all is done.

Then again we think we can do nothing, that we are helpless, if not hopeless, impotent creatures. This is simply a variation on the theme expressed: first, we expect that it is we who must do things; second, we are blind to God's power to work. So when we see the truth of our weakness and fail to look to the Lord, we do not come to realize that we can do all things in Him.

Yes, we are useless,
but in serving Him
we are strong.

In Him we can do all things, and in Him alone; for it is He alone who does all things, and apart from Him nothing is done. Never think you have accomplished anything; never believe you are without recourse. Know always that all power is in God and He wishes always to share it with those who are humble before Him, with those who live in His truth.

(Here we are like children,
 simple and pure;
 and here we are like Jesus
 as He carried His Cross.)

IV. On Finding a House of Prayer

4/25/07
St. Mark

We should be Jesus.
We are to be His Body
here on earth.
That which He did,
we should also do,
for He should work through us.

But how far from the life of Christ
sometimes our lives do seem.
Where are the miracles
He wrought
in the Church today?
Is it that we fail to follow Him,
or are these signs now
more hidden?

Certainly each day
miracles abound
in the Church
throughout the earth,
if only in the sacraments.
At every moment
His flesh and blood
are brought into our midst...
and what healing is here
and in Confession!

Perhaps it is
that we do not see this,
that we do not truly come to Him
for healing...
and so are not well able
to heal others.

Then there is the little way
of daily and humble sacrifice
in all the things in our lives.
Then there is prayer,
which reaches
from one end of the world
to the other
and can accomplish all things
in Jesus' name.
Then there is God's silent Word,
His NAME upon our still tongues...
What is more important than this,
His Presence,
and our sharing in its light?
But be there,
and all things shall be done.

4/26/07

"This is the time for my soul,"
the Blessed Mother
instructs me to say.
Now is the time for conversion,
deep conversion of heart and soul,
of mind and body, to God.
Now is the glorious moment
to consecrate ourselves
to His call.
(Perhaps now the time is upon me
 to indeed found
 this House of prayer.
 Perhaps this summer
 the Lord will bless me
 with His clear guidance
 of my life.)

2. Striving
4/27/07

I think I shall forego teaching
this summer
to concentrate entirely
on prayer and writing,
entirely on my soul
and the spiritual call of the Lord.
I pray this be in accord
with God's will
and the instruction of my Mother.
She seems to invite me to this
at this time,
though before
she would have left me to work
and seek to rise above the world.
A time of peace, for peace,
perhaps is here
(the war coming soon to an end).

Now may I but breathe for a living;
now may I find my concentration
on the presence of God,
and let this lead me
where He would take me –
to the place set aside
for me and my wife.

O Lord, I call upon your NAME
and seek to remain
in your presence.
Let your will be fulfilled
in this poor soul's life.

In his Theology of the Body, John Paul II speaks now of the Fall, of the beginning of human "history", when man goes from the state of innocence to that of concupiscence... and in this sinful moment when he sees he is naked and so is afraid, and so hides himself from God, thus comes indeed "a specific difficulty in sensing the human essentiality of one's own body" (#28, 5/28/80). Man has taken and eaten to become like God, and now sharing in that vision of angels sees he is naked, he is *not* an angel – he has a body! ... and so is harrowed to the bone.

And so shame comes,
and so we hide from God
and one another –
for we are but poor creatures.
Paradoxically, now that
we have tasted of the tree
of the knowledge of good and evil
and see like God,
we see not what God sees –
that we are made in His image
and so, very good –
but only what poor humans
can see...
only the flesh we look upon.
And so now begins the war
between spirit and body,
now that their unity
has been broken.

IV. On Finding a House of Prayer

And so Jesus comes in the form of man as if to say, "See, you are gods; I am God and you are like me." And so He comes to call us back to our original state; He comes to speak to us, even in His body, of the Father's love for us... and that we can return to Him – now we can take and eat of the bread of angels.

O save us, Lord,
from our blindness, from our fear,
from our hatred of ourselves.
(Let us accept and cherish
 our bodies;
 let them be your Body.)

4/30/07

I do seem to grow closer to understanding, to awareness, if not consciousness, of the Holy Trinity and our dear Mother. I at least think of them more, and these thoughts become prayers.

The Father is He who is always present, more real than anything of this world, anything we make by our own hands and minds. And when we still our tongue, when we cease to presume before Him... when we silence our own ways, we may begin to see that indeed He is present, more truly and really present than anything of this world.

And the blood of the Son
calls us always
to lay down our lives
to find this NAME
speaking in us.
He calls us to pray,
to be as He has been (and is),
as the One
who has laid down His life
for the salvation of all.
Our desire must indeed be
for the salvation of souls, all souls;
this is the path
the Cross shows us.
Let us be always ready to forgive,
never thinking to condemn.
O how shall we look with love
as has Christ!

And the Spirit is always ready
to give us light.
The Son sends Him forth to us
as our Advocate and guide,
as the inspiration for our lives,
leading us on right paths,
on the path He Himself trod.
And our eyes must always
be fixed
upon God's promise in hope,
ever filled with the light
of the Spirit.
And He will show us heaven,
even here, on this earth;
and we shall know it
with our Blessed Mother,
incorporated into the Lord's Body,
His holy Church.

2. Striving

5/1/07

A further word
about the Holy Spirit,
the Light of God,
the promise of the Lord,
which illumines our minds
and so our hands,
inspiring us to build the kingdom
in the Father's NAME...

As we build the kingdom,
we thus become part
of the kingdom,
building ourselves, first of all,
and most importantly,
into the kingdom of God.

Where is His Spirit, there is His light, there is His kingdom – God in a real sense *is* His kingdom: where God is, is His kingdom... We are called to live in God.

And as His Church, His Body, we are called to work. Here on earth we must utilize that gift God has given us, that is, the body. Angels have not bodies; man has. And so by our work we come to God, we come to participate in His glory, in His light, in His presence, finding the union with Him that is ours.

This seems to me quite simple,
as I have tried to make it sound:
if we do the work of God,
we are workers of God;
we are, indeed, *of God*,
as here we fulfill His call.
And if His light is in us,
illumining our work, our lives,
then His light is in us –
it cannot be otherwise.
And if His light is in us,
we are of Him, as said,
and in Him, in His kingdom,
even as we toil for Him
on this plane.

5/2/07

I do not seem to have given the Eucharist its proper or at least full weight in this discussion of a spiritual life. I have said we are called to be tabernacles, and it should be clear that the tabernacle is that which houses the Lord in the Sacrament... but somehow I seem to forget this or not to emphasize it sufficiently. Let me try to do so now.

If we receive the Lord, especially every day, how much we should become like Him, how much should we be His Houses! He comes to us, to our very bodies, and unites us with Himself and the Father.

IV. On Finding a House of Prayer

5/3/07
Sts. Philip and James

Here is obviously a great source,
the great source,
of union with God –
here God comes to us
and unites Himself to us,
even physically.
The union does not get
more real than this
on this earth.
We may often be unaware,
if not blind,
to the truth of His presence
in the Sacrament;
we may not be
sufficiently prepared
to receive Him
and the graces He would impart –
but yet, of course, He is there
and ever offering
these graces forth.

On this earth we have in the Church the Word and the Sacrament as our food for the journey through this desert. When we arrive at fulfillment of our call in the heavenly kingdom, we shall need neither of these; but here they are our means to that fulfillment, to union with God.

Let us indeed become as His tabernacles, carrying the Lord with us wherever we go, ever aware of His presence, His Word ever speaking to our hearts.

We need not fear death –
this is the realization that comes
to me in sickness this day.
We need not fear death;
we need only fear
separation from God,
and we are not
separated from God in death
because God has died.
Jesus suffered and died
(and was raised),
so suffering and death
are not without God,
not without His presence,
His love.
He leaves us not alone
but has come to be with us,
even in death.

One might indeed say
we are closest to God
in death itself –
here He shares His love with us
most intimately, most completely.
In death with God
all fear is driven from us,
and we are at peace,
complete peace.
Indeed, by death
we enter His kingdom.
O blessed doorway!
O blessed Cross!
Embrace us in your arms;
dear Lord, let us die with you.
(We shall never be separated
  from Him, brothers and sisters.)

2. Striving

Why should you fear,
foolish soul?
Jesus will never leave you,
God will never flee.
There is no place He is not...
even darkness is bright to Him.
Do you think
He will leave you abandoned?
Is this why
He has died on a cross?
Set your soul at rest.
Believe in His love.
He will be with you,
even in death.

5/7/07

Two priests, in separate homilies
on the same day (yesterday),
point out the difference
between the Shema
and Christ's call to love
as He does:
the first command is human,
the second divine.

And this crystallizes the idea,
the fact,
that we are called to be as God,
to be in union with Him.
If we love like Him who is love
what will we be
but like God Himself?

Here indeed is a *new* command,
which He gave us
in His generosity,
by His grace:
Be as I AM.
O what a tremendous,
overwhelming call!
How shall we be as God?
How can we love as He does?
We must, of course,
allow Him to live in us
and work in us,
and so to love in us.
(To what glory we are called!)

But I am so far from being
His tabernacle,
so far from carrying His grace,
His presence in my soul...
Yes, it is true.
You are polluted
and need forgiveness.
And this forgiveness, God's grace,
you will need every day.
Isn't this our cross:
that we are called to perfection,
called to God's presence,
to His love –
and this we do desire...
but always we must recognize
that we are far from His arms?
(Yet it is in this recognition
we grow.)

IV. On Finding a House of Prayer

5/8/07

There is another cross
of which I begin to become aware:
it regards prayer.
I see there is a truth
that we can do nothing,
that God does all things,
and that our prayers may even be
counterproductive.
I see that we must indeed
put everything in God's hands,
in His will...
and yet we cannot cease to pray.
And there is a rather terrible
(but beautiful)
refinement of prayer and praying
I begin to know.

It is true we must pray,
that the Lord has enjoined us
to ask all things in His Name;
but it is also true
that there comes a time
when we ask nothing,
when all is accomplished by God.
And even here, even now,
we begin to see this perfection,
and, in a sense,
the "futility" of our work.
All is always done in God,
and this truth sometimes comes
to our vision.

The Lord has told me of certain souls that if they would, they could be saved; we do all have free will, after all, and He will be known to all. And, I think, perhaps if Moses had not interceded, and the Jews had been destroyed and a race born of Moses himself... perhaps this intention of God may have been better. (And was this not accomplished by Him after all?) But I see, too, and most importantly, that there is a prayer we can always make – O Lord, transform me into your love! into the image of Jesus, the new Moses. (For love never dies and we may always grow in love.)

5/9/07

Let us love and be of love.
Let our prayers be filled with love,
be of love,
and so be of God.
Let us unite ourselves so with Him
that His will breathes in our heart,
in our heart of hearts...
for one with Him in love,
in prayer,
all our words and intentions
will be fruitful,
as He is only fruitful,
as He is only of light.

2. Striving
5/10/07

We must indeed let the Father
pray in us;
it must be His words we say,
His thoughts in our souls...
His intentions only.
O how to give our spirits over
completely to the Lord
that He might work in us
His will
in prayer?
How to ask what He desires
and see it come to fruition
before our eyes?

Love alone is the Father's will;
let it be our own.
In peace alone He dwells;
let us dwell with Him.
His wisdom shines like light,
illumining our minds...
in Him there is no darkness –
let us be children of light.

Words, words, words...
how much of this is mere words?
How shall we conform our souls
to the image of the Son?
How shall we make our home
in the Father's love?

There seems no harm,
and the possibility of great benefit,
in consecrating oneself
to the Trinity
in the following way –
to offer in prayer
one's soul to the Father,
one's heart to the Son,
one's mind to the Holy Spirit...
and one's body
to the Blessed Mother
and all the saints and angels,
that the Word of God
might be fulfilled in us
as it has been fulfilled in them.

I have discussed ideas akin to this
but have not so directly proposed
such a specific consecration.
(And indeed the idea
 has not before been so clear.)
Perhaps specific prayers
of consecration
may follow,
even in these pages.
But to order one's spiritual life
in this way –
remembering always
that the three Persons
are always One
and so, indivisible –
with specific prayers or not...
does appear to my mind
to possess
great potential blessing.

IV. On Finding a House of Prayer

5/14/07

And so, let us pray:

Father in heaven, take my soul,
infuse it
with your surpassing peace;
Jesus, my Savior, take my heart,
let it beat only with your love;
Holy Spirit, take my mind,
let it be filled with the light
of your wisdom.

Mother of God and of the Church,
into your hands
I place my broken body –
let it find strength
in the Body of Christ.

O God Most High,
let my spirit be yours alone.

Or, it seems to me,
one might more simply say:
Father, take my soul.
Jesus, take my heart.
Holy Spirit, take my mind...

Blessed Mother, take my body.

It is our second
wedding anniversary
and the feast of St. Matthias,
and my wife and I are at the shrine
of Our Lady
Queen of the Universe
(in Orlando, Florida).
Here I hope to complete,
by God's grace
and Mary's intercession,
the organization
of the book or books
I've been writing
on the Divine NAME
and on the Most Holy Trinity
and the Four Corners
of the Universe...
and the founding
of a House of prayer.

But on this day I should reflect
on my relationship
with my wife, Sylvia,
and perhaps how our marriage
is part of this spiritual life.
Generally, we pray together,
though we must still draw closer,
if not into oneness,
in our spiritual lives.
Are we doing so?
I pray we are,
though I see many failures
in this regard,
particularly on my part.
And so, just how all shall work out
yet remains unclear to my vision.

2. Striving

I should like us always to pray together, to have our hours completely coincide, much as they do in a religious house. But this is not possible, for my wife is working full time (three twelve-hour nights a week). Yet even when there is the time, I often find my throat too weak to speak aloud with her our prayers.

So questions certainly remain – one is whether such complete coincidence is the Lord's will (for it is not so in all orders, and among most hermits); another is how my throat shall heal. (Is this a call to greater silence?)

5/15/07

Question persists also regarding my hermitage. It arises especially here where I am far from my domicile. It is a question of stability. How stable ought I be?

I think of Benedict's reproach of his sister when she asked him to remain outside his cell so they could pass the night in spiritual conversation. He was adamantly against it, but she appealed to the Lord, who granted her prayer. (Here perhaps is the interplay of love and discipline which my wife and I seem called to.)

I do not like to be away from my apartment and my routine of prayer and work. When I am, I usually get sick. Should I be more adamant about remaining closer to my hermitage, the physical house the Lord provides? Or does such time away, along with the stress it brings, but provide means for me to realize the importance of the body as hermitage, that this hermitage is primary?

(It was part of my penance, too, to enjoy this vacation... I cannot do this easily, and am often lost as to how.)

What would Francis or Benedict
do at Disney World?
I find myself called
to pray for the salvation
of all souls.
Perhaps such work
is part of being a hermit in the city.
I should, I think,
rather be a hermit
in the wilderness...
but perhaps this is the suffering
the Lord desires for me.
But oh the distractions!
the lack of peace.
Is it really a call and a challenge,
or but a temptation?
(Help me this day
  to better pray, O Lord.)

IV. On Finding a House of Prayer

5/16/07

Azariah stood up
in the fiery furnace
and prayed to God
for the exiled Israelites;
Paul in prison prayed and sang
to the Lord.
And so we must ask –
where is it God does not exist?
And where should we not
call upon Him?

The basic truth
that God is everywhere
and in control of all things
must be duly discovered
and lived.

It does seem this may be
the reason
for my being here in Orlando,
and perhaps for being
a hermit in the city:
to pray for all souls
and bring the silence of God
to all places.
For none is beyond His reach,
and there is no place He is not.
And if we can bring His silence
to the noise and distraction
of this place,
of this fallen world,
perhaps some may be saved
and we ourselves fulfill
the Lord's will.

A key is that when the fire is upon us, when suffering comes and darkness threatens to overwhelm our souls, to do as Azariah and pray not so much for ourselves but for others, and, of course, always first praise the Lord.

Perhaps there will be invisible souls, hermits called by the Lord, simply to be among the people with a prayer. There seems to be in this something of Vatican II's universal call to holiness and its desire to empower the laity, though perhaps in a more intentional fashion.

5/17/07

It is Ascension Thursday,
though it is not celebrated today
in this diocese
(nor most in the U. S., it seems).
This grieves my soul,
but the Spirit brings comfort.

The priest reminds us
to begin tomorrow
our Novena to the Holy Spirit,
to ask for His gifts
that we might be holy.
And I begin to ask
even during Mass,
and find His light filling my mind
with thoughts of the Trinity
and the interaction of the Persons.

2. Striving

I ask for blessings
upon my writing,
giving it to the Lord –
and also upon my relationships
and my prayer...
I see that the heart
is the center of human life,
that we cannot escape humanity,
interaction with others,
for we are always human.
Our prayer is for humanity
and our work always for others.
And though we might seem
to be able to separate ourselves
from work and prayer
(though this, too,
 is not really possible),
we can never separate ourselves
from our humanity, from others.

And this is why Jesus is the Person most familiar to us – He is human, like us (intentionally so). But always where one is, so are the others.

And it occurs to me that different races may be closer to a different Person – the Red Man to the Father, the Creator; the Yellow Man to the Spirit, our Guide; the Black Man, who is most human (the heart), closest, as all humans, to Jesus and His Blood... and the White Man to Mary, His Mother, and so to the Church, the Body of Christ, which is called into perfect union with God.

Let them work in all your life.

I should note here that as one might in prayer consecrate the parts of one's being (soul, heart, mind, body) to the different Persons (I note here Mary is a "person", as with us all, only by adoption; *she is not God* but first of the saints), one might do the same with one's prayer, marriage/ human relationships, work, and daily life:

O Father, pray in me.
Dear Son, move me
to love others.
Holy Spirit, guide my hand
in work.
Mother Mary, all my day
I consecrate to God through you.

Do not be afraid to give all to God.

5/23/07

A few other points were brought to the fore in my time in Florida.

I see that the three stages of the spiritual life – the purgative, illuminative, and unitive – can be rather clearly applied to the three Persons of the Trinity: it is Jesus who comes to purge us, to save us from our sins; it is the Spirit who illumines our way, by whose light we are guided in this world; it is the Father with whom we are called to unite, for He is always our ultimate goal.

IV. On Finding a House of Prayer

Regarding carrying God's silence
everywhere and at all times,
and praying for the salvation
of all souls:
one can perhaps at least practice
moments of silence
each place one enters,
bringing the Lord's peace
to every house.
These moments can be keys.
They need not take long,
and no one need notice us do it.
In each place – stores, churches,
airplanes, amusement parks,
the streets...
stop a moment and pray in silence
the Father's NAME
for the salvation of all there.
(And so all places thus become
 houses of prayer.)

The journey did emphasize for me
that it is the hermitage within
that matters.
We truly must carry
the silence of God
wherever we are.
It must be found in us and of us;
the place is not important.
Though the place,
the hermit's house,
may serve the silence of God,
it is in our bodies, in our souls,
the Spirit of God must dwell –
we must indeed be
His tabernacles,
His temple.

5/24/07

It is indeed the hermitage within,
the spirit within the heart of man,
that matters.
Truly we are ourselves to be
temples of the Holy Spirit.
May the Spirit dwell in our hearts,
in our heart of hearts,
that we might in body and soul,
heart and mind,
be a tabernacle for the Lord.

(On this seventh day of the
Pentecost Novena, let us pray for
the Spirit's indwelling, and so the
indwelling of the Trinity.)

5/25/07

And ultimately it is to be
children of light
to which we are called.
It may be helpful
to conceive an order
which recognizes the four corners
of the universe
and the Three Persons
who are One,
but ultimately all is one
and we are but one –
we are children of the light of God,
living in His Spirit.

2. Striving
5/26/07

Kneeling before a statue
of St. Anthony,
the Child Jesus in his arms,
I sense such purity,
such innocence,
such simplicity,
which is our call.
All questions and doubt flee
and there is peace,
peace in the gentle light
of the Spirit.
We must indeed be as a child
before our heavenly Father.

And now that I find
the hermitage within,
now that I become a temple,
a tabernacle of the Lord
in myself, my body and soul,
I wonder about how
to join with my wife
as a tabernacle together,
how to be a *married*
hermit in the city.
Certainly I must better recognize
that she is
a temple of the Spirit herself,
and treat her more so as such...
and pray the Lord unite us,
that He make us one
as He is One,
Father, Son, and Holy Spirit.

It is the eve of Pentecost, and two years since I was married (the second anniversary day for my wife and I – the first being the 14th of May). And, of course, the Pentecost Novena ends and the Church is born.

O Lord, let us be born into your Church! Let us grow and flourish in your House!

(I note that my second wedding proposal, the one that was fully accepted, was on Nov. 9, the feast of the Dedication of St. John Lateran, the cornerstone church which houses the Chair of Peter... the first proposal was St. Joseph's feast day, March 19.)

I believe, I must believe,
that my wife and I
and this order of the Divine NAME
and these hermits in the city,
will be accepted
and find place in the Church,
that not only will my wife and I
as individual souls
and together in marriage
be as temples of the Lord,
tabernacles of our God,
but that this life I propose
will find fertile ground,
perhaps in this diocese
or in another.

IV. On Finding a House of Prayer

Now, this summer, I pray,
I must finish this proposal,
this book on this order,
that it might be submitted
to the archbishop
for his approval.

I have no more to write now.
God bless us!
God bless all souls
set on serving Him
in this world
and in the next.
(Happy Pentecost!)

6/7/07
epilogue

First, our soul must be a tabernacle, must hold the presence of God, carrying always His peace in us... for then our bodies will be a temple – it is the tabernacle which makes the church holy.

Then we can build our hearts into an altar, an altar of sacrifice for others, for all, for the salvation of souls... Christ's blood pouring forth.

And let our minds be as the lampstand, the perpetual light which illumines the temple, which stands beside the altar and by the tabernacle, illumining God's presence in us, and our sacrifice, even unto eternity.

2. Striving
7/11/07
St. Benedict

MOSES

to whom YHWH spoke His NAME

was

"the meekest man on the face of the earth" (Nm.12:3) –

indeed, let us be as children before our Father...

It is he to whom

"the LORD used to speak...face to face" (Ex.33:11),

for He had given him His NAME.

——— ——— ——— ——— ——— ——— ———

4 Final Words

1) I am naming the silence –
   God's NAME is contemplation itself.
2) I am founding an order,
   in which all souls may find a place.
3) I am seeking a House of Prayer
   for my wife and I.
4) I pray that House may contain
   the Sacrament.

****

8/24/07
St. Bartholomew

Let Him be perpetually adored in the temple of our hearts;
may His NAME be spoken always
in the holy of holies.

Other Books by James Kurt

Our Daily Bread:
Exposition of the Readings of Catholic Mass –
A page of writing for every Mass of the liturgical calendar for the Roman Rite; reflections drawn from the readings. 727 pp. 2004. w/ imprimatur.
Our Daily Bread: Lent – 86 pp. 2019. w/ imprimatur.

Prayers to the Saints (Updated) –
A page of prayer to each saint on the General Roman Calendar for the U.S.A.
237 pp. 2019 (original 2007). w/ imprimatur.

"TURN and Become like Children":
Refuting the Presumed Contradictions of the Jerusalem Bible
Old Testament Commentary –
A case study recounting the problems afflicting modern biblical scholarship as exemplified in the JB. 188 pp. 2019.

"Into Your Hands…":
Distillation of the Letters of Fr. Jean-Pierre de Caussade –
Reflections of the profound counsel of Fr. de Caussade to embrace the Cross and find the Lord's will (and joy) even in our greatest sufferings. 82 pp. 2019.

Remembrance of Things Present –
A mystical work seeking the presence of the LORD in the moment, where He dwells at all times. 100 pp. 2018. w/ imprimatur.

Two Books: Paradox and the Christian Faith /
  Hippie Convert –
The apparent contradictions of the Faith are explained for those who seek wisdom; and a member of the flower generation addresses true love and peace, in poetic form. 238 pp. 2016/2019. w/ imprimatur.

Lines of Grace: Meditations on Verses of Holy Scripture,
The Stations of the Cross, and The Most Holy Rosary –
A Catholic devotional especially for the encouragement of the practice of plenary indulgence. 195 pp. 2016.

Christian Vision of the Old Testament –
Synopsis and exhortation; faith-filled overview of all books of the Old Testament as prefiguration of Jesus, with a focus on the prophetic nature of God's Word. 273 pp. 2013/2019. w/ imprimatur.

Blessed Guilt (A Universal Conversion Story) –
On the life-giving repentance found in Jesus' blood; vaguely autobiographical but without particulars, thus making it a universal story of conversion.
119 pp. 2013. w/ imprimatur.

Chapters of the Gospels –
Exposition of the four gospels, chapter by chapter; in the style of *Our Daily Bread*.
114 pp. 2009. w/ imprimatur.

The Most Holy Trinity and The Four Corners of the Universe –
A collection of writings on the Trinity and its reflection in Creation; founded upon the Shema. 300 pp. 2008. w/ imprimatur.

Turn of the Jubilee Year: A Conversion Song –
Autobiographical depiction of vocation search through pilgrimage to Medjugorje and stays at a hermitage or two. 230 pp. 2004.

Songs for Children of Light: Ten Albums of Lyrics –
White on black conceptual work with simple line drawings for each song.
150 pp. 2003.

silence in the city –
Short contemplative poems; moments of divine silence in the midst of city life.
148 pp. (74 pieces). 2003.

author's website:
www.writingsofjameskurt.org

podcasting site:
www.hermitinthecity.libsyn.com

www.ingramcontent.com/pod-product-compliance
Lightning Source LLC
Chambersburg PA
CBHW052017070526
44584CB00016B/1792